IDENTITY OF THE RELIGIONS CALLED DRUIDICAL AND HEBREW

First Edition 1829
John Nimmo

New Edition 2021
Edited by Tarl Warwick

COPYRIGHT AND DISCLAIMER

FOREWORD

This short work is essentially a comparison of linguistics, stone remains, and ritual history, seeking to evince the theory that there was a connection between the Druids, the Hebrews, and various other groups through time- including Sanskrit-speaking Eastern areas, the Etruscans, and others. The progenitor religion which branched into these vaguely divergent practices is not named, but rather speculated, as some contemporary works did.

The theory is compelling, but has fallen out of favor lately in favor of the belief that roughly similar practices- even when linguistically overlapped- arose entirely separately, or only with contact much later, in the time of the height of the Roman Empire, etc. The crude monuments of further antiquity were slowly replaced with statuary, and the pagan practices mentioned are lamented in their slow denigration- from a sort of high priestly ritual system, to mere bard-dom and the waning of folk tales, in the 19th century, with its slow move towards more organized civilization. A few of the archaeological references herein have been discredited- others remain debated even now, almost two centuries later.

This edition of "Religions Called Druidical and Hebrew" has been carefully edited for format and content. Care has been taken to retain all original intent and meaning.

IDENTITY OF THE RELIGIONS CALLED DRUIDICAL AND HEBREW

To the literary and theosophical society of the University of London:

GENTLEMEN,

Allow me to offer to your notice a Volume on a subject, which I know will be interesting to you, I cannot omit this opportunity of congratulating you on the flourishing state of your Society; arising, I am convinced, from the noble objects to which it so unremittingly directs its attention- the stripping Literature and Science of the odious trammels, with which Pedants and Scholastic Tyrants have so sedulously and so cunningly enveloped them.

I have the honor to be,

GENTLEMEN,

Your obedient and faithful Servant,

THE AUTHOR.

London, 7th Sept. 1829.

RELIGIONS CALLED DRUIDICAL AND HEBREW

PREFACE

Before a reader, commences a work on any subject, he in general expects to find some account of it, either brief or diffuse, clear or obscure, in a Preface or Introduction, To meet the general expectations on this point, this page is devoted, with the hope, that though short, it may answer the end desired.

To escape the charge of plagiarism, the Author acknowledges his obligations to every writer on the subject, ancient or modern, with whose productions he is acquainted. The manner, in which he has attempted to prove the object of the title-page, is, in short, an examination of the different rites among the Druids and Hebrews, Their conceptions of the Deity are exhibited, and, shewn to be alike. Both cultivated grove worship and adored the oak; the temples of both were of a circular form, like that of Stonehenge; raising up lithoi were common to both; cairn or vestal fires were lighted, with similar intentions, in Judea and in Britain; Bel, Moloch, the serpent, and bull, were, equally, adored by both; both were believers in magic, and in the magical incantation of teraphim. The Jew and Druid, equally, believed in metempsychosis, offered human and other sacrifices, buried their dead, and measured time in the same manner- their hierarchy existed exactly alike both in the East and West; from these arguments, the near relation of the Hebrew and Druidical religions is proved.

Besides the existence of these customs among the Israelites and Britons, they are shewn to have prevailed in Egypt, Canaan, Carthage, Persia, Arabia, and Babylon; among the Gymnosophists, Bonzes, Hindus, Umbrians, Etruscans, and, in Italy and Greece; thereby, demonstratively proving the oriental origin of the western religion, and, its identity with that of the Israelites. Such are the arguments employed in the Work; as they are, they are given to the world, with the hope, that, on such a hidden and mysterious subject as this, the indulgence may be granted, which numerous faults and many frailties require. It cannot but be expected, that every human production will have its imperfections.

THE IDENTITY OF THE DRUIDICAL AND HEBREW RELIGIONS

The religion of mankind immediately after the flood, appears from ancient writers to have been pure theism. It continued to, predominate for several ages after that catastrophe, experiencing but very slight changes from the variety of vicissitudes to which it was exposed. The sole surviving family of that vast mass of human beings which had been so lately and so tragically destroyed, followed the religious opinions of their ancestry, and firmly believed in the same doctrines as the first inhabitants of the former world. The extreme age to which men lived in those times, rendered this effect much easier to be produced. It only required to pass through the hands of two or three individuals, so that traditional opinions were very unlikely to receive any great addition, or suffer much from detraction. The religion of the first man was pure theism; and if no revelation had intervened, the religion of the family which escaped the deluge must necessarily have had a near alliance to the same. But both sacred and profane history aver, that immediately after the cessation of the waters, the Deity was pleased to continue for a time those especial exhibitions of himself, which would have led the inhabitants of the new world to this doctrine, had they never heard the traditions of their fathers. In sacred history, whenever the Almighty appears to man, he declares himself to be one God, and forbids the worship of more than himself. Such was the religion immediately after the flood, and such was the religion of the great propagator of the Hebrew belief.

A comparison of the religion of the ancient Israelites with that of the Druids is attended with many obstacles. Little is known of the latter directly, and it is but by collecting from various sources, that any tolerably accurate account can be obtained, sufficiently diffuse for the purpose. The Pentateuch contains the fullest account extant of the practices of the ancient Hebrews; but it is in vain that a similar history of the Druids is sought for. It is only by comparing the recorded practices of the ancient Israelites with the remaining relics of Druidical customs, that any thing like identity can be established: but if it can be proved, that all the customs and opinions of the Hebrews were Druidical, both by internal and foreign evidences, then we must conclude that the religions of both nations were alike.

A vast diversity of opinions has been held, all over the world, with regard to the nature of the Deity. Almost all the Greek philosophers thought differently on this point. In antiquity it was not so. The hypotheses of succeeding years seem to have originated with the additions made to the first religion. In Egypt, in Phoenicia, in Canaan, in Persia, and in all the past, one doctrine originally prevailed. To show that this same doctrine was common in Europe and the West, forms a part of the present inquiry. The Druidical religion was followed by most of the inhabitants of the European world; and if it ever can be demonstrated, that the oriental Hebrew and the western Druid adored one and the same God, it will go far to prove that the two buildings commenced upon a similar foundation were erected on a similar plan.

The attributes of the supreme God of the Hebrews were, that though they believed surrounding nations to be under the especial governance and direction of very gods, yet they thought Jehovah Adonai, their Lord, was greater than all. (Exod. xv. 11.) That they thought other nations were governed by other gods, is plain from what Jephthah said to the king of the Amorites: "Wilt thou not possess what Chemosh thy god hath given thee?" etc. Adonai was far superior to any of these. As Creator of all things, they revere him; as Lord of the earth, they adored him. He filled immensity, and extended beyond the boundaries of space. Though a spirit, and invisible, yet he deigned at certain intervals to exhibit himself to mortal eye. Sometimes he appeared as a still small voice; then he rode on a cherub, and flew on the wings of the whirlwind; his head was clad in light, his feet embraced the gloomy darkness. He was the invigorating spirit, the life of all things. He spoke and creation arose from chaos. Terrible majesty was his clothing; he was omnipotent in power, excellent judgment, and, regarding his attributes; inscrutable to man.

The chief Deity Of Druidism had very similar attributes. Lactautius, speaking of the God of Pythtagoras, defines him, "Animus per universas mundi partes, omnemque naturam commeans atque diffusus, ex quo omnia quae nascuntur animalia vitam carpiunt." Or, as Dr. Collyer has paraphrased the passage: "God is Neither the object of sense, nor subject to passion; but invisible, only intelligible, and supremely intelligent, in his body he is like the light, and in his soul he resembles truth. He is the universal Spirit that pervades and diffuseth itself all over nature; all beings receive their life from him. There is but one God, who is not, as some ate apt to imagine, seated above the world beyond the orb of the universe; but, being himself all in all, he sees the beings that fill his Immensity. The only principle, the light of heaven, the father of all; he produces every thing, he orders and disposes everything; he is the reason, the life, and the motion of all beings."

These were the attributes of the God of the Druids. They believed that the Deity was the source of life, and giver of good. They defined his duration as eternal, and gave him omnipotence as his power. When compared, the God of Pythagoras and the Druids has the very same attributes as the God of the Hebrews. The romantic style of luxuriance, and the fanciful rioting of an oriental mind, may have painted in more vivid colors the God of the East, than the more simple and unvarnished descriptions of the God of the West; but when both statements are stripped of their native decorations, the Oriental and the Occidental Deity appear as one. One God, the creator, preserver, and ruler of all things, the life and soul of the world, who endures forever, and exists throughout space.

The names given to the Supreme Being by the Druids and

Hebrews point out in a still more definite manner the identity of the two Deities. The Hebrews were accustomed to adore God under the title of Baal. "Thou shalt call me no more Baal." (Hosea, ii. 16.)

With the Druids, Bel was the supreme God Saddai, the Almighty, was another title of the Hebrew Divinity; it likewise had its synonym in the Western world, for the word Seadah had exactly the same meaning, and was applied as a name of Bel.

The sacred name of the Lord YHVH had likewise its equivalent term among the British Druids: *Hu* was an epithet of Bel, signifying the self-existent being, he that is; and coinciding with Plato's term. The similarity in sound of the two names, and the near relation between "He that is," and "I am that I am," must strike the most careless.

Such were the ideas entertained by the Hebrews and the Druids. None can deny that the Being to whom they are given is the same; and this forms a very strong argument, though by no means the strongest that the Druidical and Hebrew religions were very similar to each other.

The manner of adoring the Supreme Being is the next, subject to be considered: though two nations may adore the same divinity, yet it does not follow that their religions are alike.

By the term religion, is generally meant the rites employed in adoration; and it is only when the identity of these rites is proved, that the identity of the religions is supposed. The great similarity existing between the Druidical and Hebrew rites will perhaps appear from the subsequent facts. Grove worship was equally prevalent among the Hebrews as among the Druids. In the deep recesses of ancient forests there are charms unknown in the open plains. A religious awe rests upon the mind. The whisper of the winds through the moss-grown oaks, the rustling of the leaves, and the solemn sound of birds in the thickets, the soft murmuring of the cadent waters conspiring with the unbroken solitude of the scenery, and the coolness of the airs- arouse all the somber feelings of the soul, and make it seem as though in the presence of Deity. There is a thrill of devotion felt in the breast, the bosom heaves but to utter praise, as all around seems to indicate a fervor of devotion which could but be induced by the superior sanctity of the place. It was in these recesses that the primal priesthood of the second world believed the Almighty to have taken up his Especial abode. It was here that, in their mystic rites the rural Druids of Britain taught their votaries the Worship of the true God. They were Well aware of the aptitude of the place; they were Well aware of its bewitching enticements.

Under these impressions, and under the same ideas, "Abraham planted a grove in Beersheba, and called there on the Lord, the everlasting God."

In after times, when the family of Abraham had greatly increased, and had left their native country, journeying northward to take possession of the land promised to their ancestors, they were strictly commanded to cut down the groves of the people whom they destroyed. (Exod. Xxxiv, 13.) Their kings in numerous instances worshiped in groves, though the practice had then been debased and become idolatrous, yet it sufficiently shows that the custom had formerly been prevalent.

The purest religion, as time passes on, is everyday liable to be corrupted. The common people must have a memento to keep their minds some idea of the being they adore. Even among civilized Christians, though there be no carved or graven image, yet how many figure to their imaginations the Deity under some terrestrial shape, whether human or inanimate! In different religions this has always occurred. While the fierce Mussulman crowns the towering tops of the minaret with the rising crescent, the Christian hangs a golden cross around his neck to keep in his remembrance what happened on Calvary. So it was with the patriarchal religion of the Druids and Hebrews. Conceiving the God they adored to be omnipotent, eternal, the giver of all life; and finding all these attributes concentrated in the highest perfection among earthly things in one tree, they adored the oak as the symbol of the Deity. The Lord God appeared to Abraham by the oak of Moreh. (The word should be translated *oak*, not plain as in our version. See Gen. Xii. 6.) He pitched his tent by an oak tree, and invited his visitors to sit in its shade, as the most honorable place he could offer them. (Gen. Xviii. 4.) Jacob, his descendant, adored the God of his fathers through the same medium as his fathers. (Gen. Xxxv, 8.) He buried his dead beneath an oak. The mystic adoration of the oak survived after many centuries had elapsed. Joshua, when the Almighty had declared his will to the people, took a stone, and raised it up "under an oak that was by the sanctuary of the Lord." (Joshua, xxiv, 26.) From which it is very evident that Joshua supposed the Deity to be more especially present beneath the shade of the oak. Gideon, likewise, saw the Lord of angels sitting beneath. an oak, at Ophrah, (Judges vi, 11.) and he set food before him; and there he prayed unto the Lord his God. Other passages in the ancient writings of the Jews might be cited; but these are quite sufficient to establish the point, that their ancestors had a mystic veneration for the oak; much the same as that which prevailed among the Greeks in the time of Homer for the oaks at Dodona, of which a very fair paraphrase may be found in Pope's translation.

The very name of the Druids has been derived by some from their worship under the oak (from the Greek for *an oak*). This, however, is very liable to objection; for long before the Greek language was invented, the Druids adored the Deity under the symbol of an oak. All authors, both ancient and modem, agree in stating the fact of Druidical rites being performed either under a single oak, or in the depths of forests of oak. Pliny, in his *Natural History,* (lib. xiv. cap. 44) mentions the high esteem which the Druids had for the oak. "They do not perform the least religious ceremonies without being adorned with garlands of its leaves." Maximus Tyrius says, that all the Celtic nations worshiped Jupiter, whose emblem or representation among them was an oak. It was from the oak, after performing certain ceremonies, that the sacred mistletoe was cut, with a golden sickle; the plant so far-famed as the cure of all the ills of man. Even in our own times the veneration for the oak partly remains. On festivals, oak branches are carried about, with all the rural pomp and magnificence of the village- the May-pole is covered with its leaves, and the happy maidens and hinds dance round it with the same delight their fathers did thousands of years ago. (This practice was prevalent all over the world, as could easily be shewn: it, perhaps, is one of the few remaining relics of antediluvian worship.)

If, then, the Druids, in the most westerly part of Europe, and the Hebrews, in Asia, adored the same God, and worshiped him under the same similitude, is it not a very powerful argument for the identity of their religion? If the religion of Britain had been invented, without any communication with the Eastern world, why did its inventors happen to have, not only the same notions of the Deity, but likewise to adore him under the same similitude. In Europe, the oak might be the most prominent object of worship; but in Asia, how many other trees are there which, with much more propriety, might have been substituted? Would not the eternal cedar, or other odoriferous trees of the Oriental world, have given a more pleasing idea to the sun-burnt Asiatic of his God. There is nothing so demonstrative of the antediluvian origin of both the Druidical and Hebrew religions, as this adoration of the oak.

In the first ages of the world, and down until comparatively modern times, the Deity was adored only in the open air. "It was held unlawful to build temples to the gods, or to worship them within walls or under roofs." (Tacitus, de Morib. Germ.) The priests of those times held it as a perfectly ridiculous idea to attempt to confine the Deity in a covered house. Their notions of his ubiquity led them to suppose that it was unlawful: the only temple they gave their God was the universe, the heavens were the covering, the earth its altar. When they had experienced any signal favor, or received any gift at the hands of their deity, their usual custom was to erect a stone, in remembrance of the blessing; and the ground on which such stones were placed was supposed to be hallowed. Their astronomical acquirements had taught them that certain stars rose when spring, summer, autumn, and winter, commenced; their acquaintance with different cycles, and other astronomical occurrences led them to commemoration them by raising up these stones, which were generally ranged in a circular form; in process of time, hollow caverns were substituted, having painted or other representations on their roofs of the concave of heaven; and it was, perhaps, from this sort of adoration, that Sabaeism, or the adoration of all the stars, began.

It is with the circular temples that we have to do at present; they abound in England, and other parts of Europe. The most ancient account of them is to be found in the book of Exodus, (xxiv. 4.) "And Moses rose up early in the morning, and builded an altar under the hill, and twelve pillars, according to the twelve tribes." The manner in which these circular temples were erected, may be fully gathered from other parts of the Pentateuch. (Deut. xxvii. 2, etc.) An altar of more than one stone, probably of three, (Altars of three stones are frequent in England, and have been denominated *trilithims*.) was erected, and round it other stones were raised, which had never been touched by tools, except such as were absolutely necessary for the purpose of procuring them. They were to be entirely misshapen and raised up in the condition they were first quarried or found. These stones were covered over with plaster. On the altar burnt offerings were offered. Epiphanius says that at Shechem there was a temple built by the Samaritans of a circular form. This temple is again and again spoken of in the sacred writings. It appears extremely probable, that all the cities of refuge of which so much is said in the Scriptures, were temples erected in this circular manner. At Shechem, Jeroboam Was made king over Israel, and Rehoboam rejected; at Shechem there was a high priest; and Joshua (xxiv. 26) says, that it was the especial sanctuary of the Lord The circular temple of stones on Mount Gerizim, mentioned in Deut. xxvii. 2, (for Dr. Kennicott has shown that the true reading is Gerizim, and not Ebal) was famous among the Greeks. In all these sacred circles a custom prevailed of burying the dead bodies of such as had held superior stations among the people: "so Joseph was buried in the temple at Gerizim."

The most diffuse account of the foundation of one of these temples, is that which was erected at Gilgal, (Joshua, iv. 6). This appears to have been the grand metropolitan see of the Hebrews: they had just crossed Jordan, and, in compliance with the express command of Heaven, they erected a plain temple of twelve stones, arranged in a circle, having an altar in its center. It was at this temple that the grandest and most magnificent occurrence of the Jewish empire transpired: here Samuel changed the theocracy of the Hebrews into a monarchy, (I Sam. xi. 14); it was here that the new-made monarch invoked the Lord, before he began his first war against his Philistine neighbors; and it was here that the people assembled to celebrate all their great festivals.

Stonehenge, in England, is now universally allowed to be one of this description of temples; its stones are arranged in a circular manner, exactly like the description of those cf the Jews; and its appearance proclaims its' extreme antiquity; but its magnitude and rude grandeur declare, that the people who first raided the ponderous blocks of stone of which it is composed, were both learned and powerful. If Joshua, the Wandering warrior, with his six hundred thousand fighting men, could produce only such an insignificant temple as that at Gilgal- to what a pitch of grandeur and magnificence must the Druidical empire in Britain have arrived, before it could erect Stonehenge, Abury, and the hundreds of circular temples that covered the British Isles?

RELIGIONS CALLED DRUIDICAL AND HEBREW

Every day the magnificent relics of these remains of grandeur and antiquity are being discovered; and it is surprising, even to the accomplished philosopher of the nineteenth century, how the rude and uneducated Druid accomplished mechanical labors which would put bis utmost skill to the severest trial. In Ireland, as well. as in England, a vast number of these circles exist; but it is in the Scottish Islands that they are discovered in the finest preservation. In the Orkney Islands, at Classerniss, and various other places, they are found. In France, and on the Continent, they are to be met with; and it must be supposed that they were used for the same purpose in Europe as they were in Asia- for to what other purposes could they be applied? Joshua himself, the builder of the structure at Gilgal, appears to have anticipated this question. when he assembled the Israelites at the new temple, and said, "When your children, in future ages, shall ask their fathers what mean these stones? then ye shall let them know, that these were erected as an acknowledgment to the mighty Lord; that ye might fear the Lord your. God for ever."

Such were the intentions of the ancients in raising these circular temples. Avery little inquiry will shew how well they were calculated to obtain the end desired. The feelings of the devotee, at entering these mystic circles, must have been indescribable. The dying sounds of human sacrifices, the awful solemnity of the surrounding scenery, the vast and silent concourse of attentive people, the rude, romantic, imposing magnificence of the structure, as the. arch Druidical prophet emerged from beneath the mysterious trilithic altar, and announced to the wondering multitudes the answers he had heard in whispers from his God- the feeling of the rotary must have been intense, and almost overwhelming. These were the most ancient temples in use; and it was not until long after the Jews crossed Jordan, that Solomon, their third king, raised the first covered temple to the Almighty. (1 Kings, iii. 2.)

It has been said, that when the ancients experienced any

signal favor, or reserved any gift at the hands of their Deity, it was their usual custom to erect a stone in remembrance of the blessing; and the ground an which such stones were raised was accounted holy. In the British Islands, pillars of this description are very frequent, and are called among antiquaries lithoi. The most famous in the Western world are those which Hercules erected, or is said to have erected, at the Straits of Gibraltar. "There are in the Highlands of Scotland, and in the adjacent isles numerous obelisks, or stones set up on end, some thirty, some twenty four feet high, some higher, some lower; and this sometimes where no such stones are to be found; Wales being likewise full of them, and some there are in the least-cultivated parts of England, with very many in Ireland. In most places of the last kingdom, the common people believe these obelisks to be men transformed into stone by the magic of the Druids. This is also the notion of the vulgar in Oxfordshire, of the Rollwright stones; and in Cornwall, of the Hurles, erect stones so called; but belonging to a different class from the obelisks of which I now discourse. And indeed in every country the ignorant people ascribe to the devil or some supernatural power, at least to giants, all the works which seem to them to exceed human art or ability; while the more reasonable part are persuaded, that the erect stones of which we speak are the monuments of dead persons, whose ashes or bones are often found near them. That obelisk, if I may so call it, in the parish of Bravas, in the Island of Lewis, in Scotland, called the Thrushel stone, is very remarkable, being not only above twenty feet high, which is yet surpassed by many others, but likewise almost as much in breadth, which no other comes near. (Toland's History of the Druids.)

Mr. Brand, speaking of these obelisks, says: "Many of them appear to be much worn by the washing of the winds and the rain, which shews that they are of long standing. And it is very strange to think how, in those places and times, they got such large stones carried and erected." In Penrith churchyard there are two of these lithoi; but one at Poitiers, in France, exceeds all that we have in England, being sixty feet in circumference, and raised upon the tops of five others, though this belongs ta the kind of obelisks called cromlechs. It appears that these stones were raised up as acknowledgments to the Deity; the larger ones, perhaps, for national favors, and the lesser by private individuals.

This practice in the Oriental world was just as prevalent as in the West. Abraham (Gen. xii. 7, 8) is reported to have raised up two of these stones. Isaac, his son, (Gen. xxvi. 25) raised up another, and there called on the name of the Lord. Jacob, his son, (Gen. xxviii. 18,) raised up another, poured oil on the top of it, and called the place Beth-el, having vowed to the Lord that he would adore him here. Some have stated, that from this pillar arose all those strange accounts of the Bethyllia, or animated stones, so prevalent in antiquity. The Deity was pleased to appear to Jacob, and to designate himself as the God of Beth-el, which caused the Israelites to hold this pillar in great esteem, and perhaps might be the origin of all those fables. Jacob erected another, and called it Galeed (Gen. xxxi. 45). The practice was so common with this patriarch, that scarcely did ever any peculiar circumstance happen to him, but he erected a memorial; he buries his wife, and erects a pillar over her grave, etc. Balaam (Num. xxiii. 1) raised up these stones as altars to the Lord. Gideon built an altar to the Lord at Ohprah, (Judges, vi. 24,) and called it Jehovah-shalom. Samuel the prophet took a stone and set it between Mizpeh and Shen, saying "Hitherto the Lord hath helped us." (1 Sam. vii. 12). King Saul did the same (1 Sam. xiv. 35). Josiah, too, stood by an altar and made covenant with the Lord. From all these, it is quite evident that the practice alike prevailed both among Hebrews and Druids, These pillars might contribute much to the advancement of idolatry in the first ages. Men, after adoring the Almighty by these pillars, would next adore them as representatives of him; and, lastly, would look upon them as gods themselves. Such was the case when Christianity first dawned in England; and even after the conversion of the people, the primitive missionaries, finding how loath they were to leave off adoring these senseless blocks, cut crosses upon them, that they might have a little more of Christianity in their appearance.

This capital expedient has had at least one good effect: it has preserved them for the curious antiquary to gaze upon. It was not only among the Hebrews and Druids, that these pillars were adored as gods. The Bacchus of the Thebans was a pillar. The god of the Arabians is reported by Maximus Tyrius to have been a square block of stone. Such likewise was the first Jupiter of the Romans, who was carefully concealed by the priesthood from the people; but by many is supposed to be still in existence at Rome, having been procured, perhaps, from ancient Troy, where it once, stood as the famous Palladium. When Jacob had the conference with Laban, mentioned in Gen. xxxi. 45, he ordered all his attendants to gather stones, and form them into a pile or heap, which he called Galeed. The two patriarchs then invoked God to witness, the God to whom they had erected the pile, to judge between them; and if either party passed beyond the heap with any hostile intention towards the other, they then called on the Deity to punish him with the utmost severity.

The Druids in Europe carried this custom of building altars of loose stones, and lighting fires on them, to a very great extent. All over Britain they had these altars or cairns erected, of a gigantic size; and on the eve of May-day they lighted fires in honor of Bel, or Baal; each of these fires was in the immediate vicinity of some other, and could be seen from it. The grandeur of the sight, when the fires were all lighted, must have been magnificent; the whole kingdom in one blaze, welcoming the returning Spring. Such were the rites of the ancient Druids. The homely altar built by Jacob and Laban, compared with the cairns of the Britons, serves only to exhibit the greatness to which this early priesthood had attained.

The worship of Bel, Baal, Belepus, or Balanos, was much cultivated in Palestine. Originally, Baal was a name for Jehovah

Adonai; but, when the Israelites became idolaters they served other deities, under the title of Baalim, and then they were not allowed to invoke the true God under the title Baal, (Hosea, ii. 16.) That Baal was the Deity of the first patriarchs, is attested by numerous passages, and by the manner of adoration. This worship bad grown so much upon them, and was so very extensive, that it was never entirely exterminated from the people. So soon as one king had done what he could to destroy it, another re-introduced it. The various vicissitudes it underwent merely served to exhibit, by the violence of its expiring struggles, the strength it had attained. It is but by time and case, that from a helpless infant man becomes powerful and strong, so that even in his decline he is able to exert those gigantic energies he sometimes does; and this worship of Bel must have long been cultivated, and widely extended, before it could make such resisting efforts. Its roots must have penetrated deeply, and spread widely, to have enabled its branches to withstand in so extraordinary a manner the assailing winds which would have overwhelmed it had it been but the produce of a day.

In the book of Judges it is expressly stated, that Baal, and not the Lord, was the object of adoration among the Hebrews, and ever after there is a distinction made between the true God and Baal. It is quite apparent that some change must have taken place between the time of Abraham and that of Moses. Probably, the Hebrews, by going down into Egypt, had added to the pure rites with which they worshiped their God, the impure and idolatrous customs of the chief deity of the vulgar Egyptians, (There was a vast difference in Egypt between the religion of the people and that of the priests; with the people, Osiris was the chief god; but with the priests, Ptha was the supreme and only lord.) Osiris, and had entered into all the abominations of Tauric worship. Moses, when he gave them a new religion, (No one, I am sure, can conscientiously suppose that the religion of the patriarchs, and that of the Jews after the giving of the law, were the same. The old patriarchs worshiped Baal, sacrificed in high places, adored in groves, planted oaks, intermarried with their immediate relatives;

all which were forbidden by Moses. In almost every grand point of religion, the patriarchal and Mosaic dispensations vary. I found that these enormities had attained to such a height, that, to eradicate them, it was necessary to put down the worship altogether. They no longer adored the true God under the title which their fathers had given him; they had profaned his sacred name by prostituting it to his creature the Sun. Adonai was no longer the invisible, inscrutable object of their adoration; his ineffable title had not only been given to the Sun, but they had actually plunged themselves still deeper in disgrace, and had, with daring lip, profaned it by bestowing it on that most scandalous of all the heathen deities, Baal-peo, or Priapus.

Such a state of things called loudly for alteration. A person of the discretion and experience which Moses must have acquired during the eighty years which had passed over his head, would soon perceive, that to cut off the excrescences was a much harder task than to give a new religion. In this he was led by the declared will of the Almighty; and, aided by such an omnipotent ally and friend, he delivered to the people the purest religion which had yet appeared upon earth. Baal no longer was the name of the Lord- sacrifices in high places were abolished- groves were no more to be planted; for, now, the whole system underwent an entire change.

Bel, when the Druids fell from their original purity of manners, became, as it did among the Israelites, a title of Phoebus, Apollo, or the Sun, and as such was worshiped by them as one of the most powerful gods. The grand festival to this deity was on the eve of the first day of May, when the Sun entered Taurus, and Spring began. On that evening, in all Druidical countries, the cairn fires were lighted, and the mystic orgies of the apostate religion were celebrated amid the dying groans of human sacrifice, and the rumbling noises of the adoring throngs. As the Druidical priests uttered in dark whispers the prophecies of the ensuing harvest, and ruled the multitudes by the tottering, of the Logan stones, sacrifices were offered, and .every thing was performed that could make the pageant showy; magnificent, and grand. Though the practice a in a great measure now lost, yet the name still remains; the Irish still call the eve of the first of May La Bealteim. The same name still attached to the same eve in the Scottish Highlands; and proverbs yet exist, (Such as, "I was between Bel's two fires" etc.) which have descended from the times of our Druidical forefathers until now.

That Baal of the Hebrews, and Bel of the Druids, were the same god, no doubt whatever can exist. There is such a marked coincidence, not only in the name, but likewise in the history of both, as demonstratively proves their identity. Moloch was another god to whom the idolatrous Hebrews likewise paid their devotions. In the book of Leviticus, (xviii. 21,) they were expressly forbidden to pass their children through the fires to him. Against the adoration of this false god the strong penalties are threatened (chap, xx.) To this god, Manasseh made an offering of his children; not that he sacrificed them, but he made them pass through the fire to him. Other kings of Israel were likewise given to these abominations, but Manasseh, in particular, was entirely devoted to them, not merely outraging, as a private person, those very laws which he ought to have obeyed, but attempting, as a king, to introduce a system of religion which above all others had been condemned by the great Legislator of the Jews. He made Judah and Jerusalem to do worse than pagan heathens, who, for their idolatry, had been expelled out of the land, of which he was then the governor.

The same arguments, which were used to prove the antiquity and universality of the worship of Baal, might again be used to prove that of Moloch. Would the laws of the Jews have been so terrible, so explicit on this point, had not the people been previously much devoted to this worship, of the deity? Let anyone read the anathemas uttered against the Worship of Moloch in Leviticus, and then say whether the people to whom they were pronounced, must not at one time have been entirely the worshipers of this god.

Moloch appears to have been but an epithet or name for Baal, and is in the Old Testament, always included in the word Baalim. The priests of Moloch walked through the fire& they lighted in honor of their god, as a sort of lustration, after having slain the animal for the sacrifice, they taking the entrails in their hands, walked thrice through the fires. As Bel was the title given to the Sun of the first day of Spring, so Moloch appears to have been his title on the first day in Autumn, when his heats were supposed to be the greatest, and when, after the vernal beauties of the new year, the time approached in which the Sun was ripening, with a more direct ray, the kindly fruits of the earth. It was then that the Jews adored him as Moloch, it was then that they passed themselves and their children through the fires to him, in thankful gratitude for the benefits he was bestowing.

Caesar, in his Commentaries, lib. vi. says, "Alii immania simulacra magnitudine habent, quorum contexta viminibus membra, vivis hominibus comlpent quibus succensis circumventi flamma exanimantur homines." This has evidently an allusion to the worship of the god Mallach or Moloch, to whose deity the Druids kindled large fires about midsummer, and, with the people, leaped through them. In some instances they might have carried the practice to the lengths which Caesar mentions; but the account given by Virgil is perhaps much nearer both to the rites of Hebrews and Druids. He makes Aruns, a Gallic Druid, speak, in the 11th book of his Aeneid, to this effect:

> O patron of Saraote's high abodes,
> Phoebus, thou ruling power among the Gods;
> Whom first we serve, whole woods of unctuous pine
> Bum on thy heap, and to thy glory shine;
> By thee protected, on our naked soles
> Through flames unsinged we pass, and tread the kindled

coals:
Give me, propitious power, etc.

Here it is quite evident, that on the top of Soracte there was a cairn of Apollo, of which we read, in the book of Numbers (xxi. 8), that the Israelites, when passing through the wilderness, were dreadfully tormented with the bites of fiery flying serpents; and that Moses, to heal the people, made a copper serpent, and set it upon a pole, that whoever of the sufferers looked upon it might be healed and not die. Not that the serpent, as is elsewhere said, had any power of his own, by enchantments or otherwise, to effect this cure; but that by looking on the copper effigy, they might be put in remembrance of some attribute of the Deity, or of the Deity himself. Moses, when he first received his commission from the Almighty threw down his shepherd's crook, or rod, and it became a serpent. God had just designated himself as the self-existent, eternal Being: "I am that I am;" or, as the Arabic has it, "the Eternal, who passes not away;" or the Septuagint, "I am He who exists." All which plainly allude to the eternal existence of the Almighty: he had existed from all eternity and would exist forever.

The serpent was a sacred reptile among the Druids. They supposed its spiral coils to represent the eternal existence of the Almighty. This idea was carried to such a length, that the vulgar actually thought (and in many countries still do so), that the serpent was immortal. Serpents annually change their skin, and, after that occurrence, appear quite young again; so the idea might naturally arise from the observation of this fact. The grand metropolitan temple of the Druids at Abury, was built in the form of a serpent, with a circle on his back, to the Eternal God. The amazing length to which the avenue (which was the tail of the serpent) stretched, is surprising; and not less so is the immense mound of earth which formed the head. The circle on the back of the reptile constituted one of those temples of which we have already spoken. This must have been, when in its pristine glory, the most magnificent temple in the world. Amulets of glass are frequently found, spotted with dots arranged in a spiral form; these took their origin from a supposition that certain serpents, collecting themselves in a mass, produced a magic bubble, of which these were the representation.

So did he in Beth-el, sacrificing to the calves that he had made; and he placed in Beth-el the priests of the high places that he had made. So he offered upon the altar which he had made in Beth-el, the fifteenth day of the eighth month, even in the month that he had devised in his own heart, and ordained a feast unto the children of Israel, and burnt incense. The golden calves were standing in the time of Jehu.

Such were the golden calves that Jeroboam set up in Dan and Beth-el, and such was the avidity with which the Israelites adored them. To make no comment on their conduct in likening their Maker to the grazed ox, it may merely be asked, where and when did they come at the knowledge of Tauric worship? Did Abraham, the father of the faithful, the friend of God, bow down before the bull? Did he offer incense to it? In all probability he never did, and therefore these reprobate Israelites must have learned this species of idolatry in Egypt; for it was not only prevalent among the descendants of Jacob, but had spread even among the Druids of England. Tauric festivals were celebrated among our ancestry. On the eve of May-day all the fires were lighted on the tops of the cairns, and the whole island was in one illuminatory blaze; the people leaped through them in honor of Bel. Long poles, thence called May-poles, were erected; they were crowned with garlands, and round them the youths and maidens danced in all the pleasures of rural glee. This festival was celebrated in honor of Spring, which then commenced. The Sun entered Taurus, the bull, and all these joyous proceedings welcomed his approach, when the bull opened with his horn the vernal year. (Virg. Georg. I. V. 217.) Hence it was that the calves or bulls adored by the Israelites were golden, because gold, by its resplendent beauty, was a proper representative for the benign

RELIGIONS CALLED DRUIDICAL AND HEBREW

Sun, which then was beginning to shed his glittering beauties at the approach of spring. All nature was about to burst from the iron gloom, in which she had been held by the nipping frosts of winter. The leaves were beginning to put forth their gay beauties- in every thing was youth. The airs were cool- birds, beasts, and fishes, all heard the attractive calls of the vernal goddess. Man, endued with reason, could not be insensible to all these charms; he had not so lately felt the chilling cold of the past season, without learning to estimate the delicious luxuries of all the joyous scenery around him. The warbling sounds of the birds affected his hearing, and his sight was delighted with the enameled landscape before him. The sweet scents of the vast variety of flowers emerging from the ground, luxuriously feasted his feelings, while his taste was regaled with the collected juices of the new-born fruits. Placed under such circumstances as these, could man, a being endued with reason, be insensible to such powerful charms? No; when the beasts, and even inanimate nature, seemed all to break forth with joy, and to be dad with rejoicing, man must feel the kindly influences which governed the times. He looked up to the Sun, and, seeing in him the cause of these heavenly sensations and delightful pangs adored him, as the creature of the Being whose kindness governed the seasons, whose goodness gave the gentle Warmth; and moderated the cooling breeze, which wafted the softest fragrance of the odoriferous plants: The rise of Tauric Worship is beautifully painted in the following Stanza of a hymn to Mithras, the Sun:

> Yes, though the Sanskrit song
> Be strewn with fancy's wreaths,
> And emblems rich, beyond low thoughts refined,
> Yet heavenly troth it breathes,
> With attestation strong.
> That, loftier than thy sphere, the Eternal Mind,
> Unmoved, unrivaled, undefined,
> Reigns with providence benign.
> Since thou, great orb, with all enlightening day,

Rulest the golden day;
How far more glorious He, who said, serene,
Be and thou wast, himself unformed, unchanged,
unseen.

These were similar words to those which might be addressed to the Sun, the lord and ruler of springs by the primeval race of men; The sign of tine zodiac in which this spring quarter commenced, would be the next object of adoration I and it was thus, in honor of the fairest of the season that the Bull weed adored. To point out with still greater precision the reason why the bull was adored on the first day of May, we need but turn aside to the most ancient religion of the Persians; this, though it rather belongs to another part of this essay, we shall slightly touch upon here. Freret says, the feasts of Mithras were derived from Chaldea, where they had been instituted for celebrating the entrance of the Sun into the sign Taurus. Oromazes, Mithras, and Arimanius, were the celebrated trinity of the Persians; Mithra itself means the sun; he was a very favorite god among them. Various were the parables, fables, and tales, concerning this Mithras; a tablet representing one of them yet remains in the British Museum. It represents Mithras killing a bull- a very suitable circumstance for him to be placed in. This worship of the Mithraitic bull continues still among the descendants of the ancient Persians. When they were driven from their country by persecution, and compelled by the barbarity of the times, multitudes of them settled near Bombay and Surat, where the Hindus had given them lands, on this stipulation, that they should not sacrifice either bull or ox. They adore the Sun under the element of fire; and this is perhaps one great reason why bullocks or oxen were invariably offered in antiquity as sacrifices. To an oriental fancy there might be some similitude between Mithras killing a bull, and the fire, his representatives devouring its flesh.

Bull-baiting or fighting is a practice which originally came from the East, and is generally supposed to have been taught by the Moors to the Spaniards; but where the Moors learned it, does not appear: it is almost certain that the Spanish bull-fights are only relics of the Mithraitic worship which yet continue. The allegory of Mithras killing the bull is now forgotten and unknown; but the ceremonies of bull-fighting, which used to be practiced on the first of May, still remain.

The Roman Mithras was exactly the same as the oriental: this is proved by an altar raised to this god during the third consulate of Trajan, having on it this inscription, "Mithras deo soli invicto Mithra." Bacchus was the same deity, and the Bacchic and Tauric worship were one: the priests of Bacchus crowned themselves with ivy-leaves, and sung the most extravagant hymns to their deity, exactly in the same manner, though much more vehemently, than the inhabitants of Britain, who danced crowned with garlands round the May-pole, The worship of the one people was vulgar, rude, and wild; the worship of the other tranquil and "peaceful." That Bacchus represented the Sun, no one, after consulting the elder and better educated of the Greek and Roman writers, can reasonably doubt; so says Orpheus, in one of his hymns, speaking of Dionysius, or Bacchus, And Eumolpus in his hymns to Bacchus.

Virgil in Georg. I. Verse 5:

And you, ye splendid lights,
Who kindly shine upon our lower world,
You rule the seasons and direct the year,
Bacchus and Ceres.

There is one observation which might be made to prove that Bacchus merely rose out of a celebration of the Tauric festival: Bacchus is represented horned, and called Bugenes, or sprung from a bull. It is of no consequence to carry the parallel further, as the mythology of Bacchus has merely an obscure relation to the festivities of May-day.

RELIGIONS CALLED DRUIDICAL AND HEBREW

To point out in a more definitive manner the intimate connection between the calves of Jeroboam and the Druidical festival of May-day, it will only be necessary to view the case in an astronomical light. It has already been said that the Tauric festivities celebrated on May-day were in honor of the commencement of spring, and therefore the vernal equinox at the time when Tauric worship commenced, fell on the first day of May; or, the Sun entered the sign Taurus on that day. Every year the spring commences a little previous to which it did the year before; this arises from the recession of the equinoxes, or from a slow, revolution of the poles of the equator round those of the ecliptic. In 25,920 years the pole of the ecliptic makes one entire revolution round the equatorial pole, therefore the. equinoctial solstice occurs before the time it did the preceding year. In 73 years the precession amounts to one degree.

Therefore, if we have the equinoctial or solstitial point given in the ecliptic, at any unknown period, it is easy to discover how long that period is passed by means of the preceding considerations. This method was first proposed by Sir I. Newton, to discover, by the position of the colures, how much time had elapsed since Chiron, the centaur, lived, and thereby to ascertain the true time of the Trojan war. When Tauric worship commenced, the horns of the bull were tipped by the equinoctial colure, "he then began to open with his horns the vernal year" but the horns of the bull are now 80 degrees from the equinoctial point; and as it requires 72 years to recede one degree, 80 X 72 = 26760 years, which gives the time that has elapsed since the Tauric festival of May-day was instituted.

But Jeroboam ordained a feast on the eighth month, and the fifteenth day of the month. Now, originally, the year was supposed to consist of 12 months, each month of 30 days, the remaining five days and few minutes were brought in after a sufficient time had elapsed to complete another month. In their festivals, where they were not particular to a few minutes, the year was supposed to consist of 366 days. The fifteenth day of the eighth month falls on November the sixth. There were two festivals to Bel during the year; the first on the first day of springs the second on the first day of autumn; this last was, perhaps, consecrated to Moloch, as has been already stated, both, however, were sacred to the Sun. The year was divided into four seasons, each season consisting of ninety days. If six days be subtracted from November (these six were added to 360, the sum of the four seasons, merely to make the time come nearer to the truth), and, then, if two seasons, or 180 days, be subtracted from 360, it brings the commencement of spring, or the first Tauric festival, to the first day of May; the day, as shewn above, when the same worship was cultivated in Britain, where, like that festival, it must have been instituted at least 6760 years ago.

How is it possible that this striking coincidence could happen between the customs of two people, who, to all appearance, never had any communication with each other? How could Jeroboam, the Jewish king, adore the same God, with the same festivities, in the same manner, on the same day, that he was being worshiped in a similar manner by the distant British Druid? Chance could never effect any such occurrence. Both the festivals tally with each other in every point; it is, therefore, surely ridiculous to suppose that they were invented in the same year, and the same day of that year, (6760 years ago,) in two distant countries. Will it ever be credited, that some Druid in Europe, and some Magian in Persia, sat down on the same day of the same year, invented the same festival, in honor of the same god, with the same rites, and adored in the same manner? No, this Tauric festival goes far towards proving that the religion of the Jews and that of the Druids were alike.

But, it may be said, how can this period be given as the commencement of Tauric worship, when it is well known that the earth is very little older than 5760 years, the period assigned? But this is. only a vulgar mistake, founded upon a stupid calculation, which makes the world to be only 4004 years old, at the birth of our Savior. This period was ascertained by calculating the lives of the patriarchs, as mentioned in the Old Testament. But, to shew that the present copies of the Scriptures cannot be relied on in a chronological point of view, the received version will make the world (in 1830 A.D.) 5824 years, the Samaritan version 6075, the Septuagint 7220. Besides these great discordancies between various copies of the Old Testament, there are other internal disagreements; thus, our English translation makes the age of Terah, the father of Abraham, to be 205 years, whereas, upon adding up the data, namely, 70 years before the birth of Abraham, and Abraham's age 75 when Terah died, it is plain that it makes but 145 and not 205. The. question then is which of the two is to be taken in making up the chronology of the world, 145 or 205? The ancient method of calculating by letters, rendered it very easy to make mistakes of this nature. In transcribing one copy from another, if anything were wanting to complete the demonstration of the identity of these feasts, as already given, it would be supplied by a minuter description of the rites employed: Jeroboam substituted his feast in the stead of the feast of tabernacles, but employed the same rites, that he might accustom the people to the adoration of his calves. These were, that it was to be a holy day, and kept with rejoicing and glee; no servile work was to be done thereon. Fires were to be made to the Lord, and sacrifices offered. In gratitude for the kindly ripening effects of summer, when they had gathered of the fruits of the land, they were to make a feast, to take the boughs of goodly trees, branches of the palm, boughs of the thick trees (or oak), and willows of the brook. Intertwining branches of these trees with flowers and fruits, they were to bend them into booths, and, dwelling in them, were to celebrate the time with all the gay festivity of the season. Others, carrying thick, beautiful branches to the temple, waved them to the four winds, and danced about with them in their hands, singing and chanting, "Save us O Lord." Bullocks and oxen were offered, as the people drew water out of the wells, which the priests poured forth on the altar. Do I, when writing this, describe the feast of Jeroboam, or the Druidical honors paid to May-day? Or, were they both alike?

Many have supposed, that image-worship began very early after the flood, from the circumstance of images being mentioned in the book of Genesis, as being stolen by Rachael from her father Laban. These images, as they are called in the English version, are designated by the word teraphim in the Hebrew. It is very probable that this word teraphim was derived from *rapha*, to heal or restore, and that they were *telesms*, which were supposed to have a great governance over man, for, they are emphatically called gods. That they could not all be little images, is plain from Judg. xviii. V. 14, where, they are expressly distinguished both from graven and from molten images, in three different verses. Judea abounded with these teraphim during the reign of Josiah. That they were consulted, as capable of foretelling future events, is apparent from Ezek. xxi. v. 21. And, it is very probable that Rachael stole them, that her father might not be able to discover the route of the fugitives by their assistance. The little golden *emerods* and *mice* which the Philistines pat into the ark of the Lord, belonged to the order of telesms.

From a consideration of all these circumstances, it appears that teraphim were telesms employed for various astrological purposes, and were of various descriptions, some being images, such were perhaps some of those of Laban; others amulets, like those of the Philistines, and part of Laban's. Those mentioned in Judg. xviii, V. 14, were very likely amulets. The teraphim used by the king of Babylon, as related by Ezekiel, were perhaps cylinders made of stone or metal, on which were engraved certain astrological or magical representations, used for the foretelling events.

The teraphim of the Scriptures have a very near alliance to the *Penates* of the western world. These Penates were so called from having their habitation in the innermost recesses of heaven. They are supposed to govern man entirely by their superior powers; "we can neither live, nor use our understanding without them." The Tuscans thought that they were the greatest among the gods and governed even Jupiter; some went so far as to enumerate Jupiter himself and all the other gods among them. Dionysius says that these Penates were not of any given shape or figure, some were like wooden or brass rods, in the shape of trumpets; others say they were like men with spears.

It has already been mentioned, that among the Druids there existed a species of amulets, which have been called *anguinum ovum*, or serpents' eggs; these were for preserving the person, who wore them, from all kinds of evils, and appear to have a very near alliance to the teraphim of Scripture. Magical enchantments of this nature were very common among them; Origen (Philosophoumenos) says "the Druids make use of enchantments."

It is well known that the priesthood of antiquity, in almost every part of the world, had two distinct doctrines or religions; the one sacred, and known but to themselves, the other vulgar, and taught to the people. In Egypt this was the case; for, though the priests themselves were well aware that there was but one God, they inundated the country with a numberless company of beings, which they persuaded the people were very deities. The same was the case in Greece; Pythagoras, Plato, and all the great philosophers, were well assured of the unity of the Divine Being, though none of them except Socrates had honesty enough to tell the people the truth. The Romans served lords many and gods many, yet Cicero, and some others of their sages, were persuaded that these existed, as divinities, but in the deluded fancy of the common people.

The Druids were believers in the metem- psychosis or transmigration of souls, as Caesar says, "In primis hoc volunt persuadere, non interire animus, sed ab aliis post mortem transire ad alios." (It is a very favorite maxim of the Druids, that souls do not die, but pass, after the death of one body, into another). Upon this point, indeed, the Druidical and Israelitish faith may seem to differ; for this, which was a favorite maxim of the Druids, cannot be found among the Israelites. But, the first thing to be discovered is what is meant by transmigration of souls, or metempsychosis. The Druids, like other priests, had two doctrines, a sacred and a vulgar. No doubt Caesar's account of the metempsychosis belonged to the vulgar religion, while the true meaning involved some mystic knowledge of the natural history of man.

Serranus, the French translator of Plato, supposes the doctrine of the metempsychosis to be mythic, and to have some allusion to future resurrection. Ficinus asserts that it is allegorical, and must be understood of the manners, affections, and. tempers of man. That it was allegorical, there can be very little doubt. A man of the learning of Pythagoras, who was skilled in all the wisdom of Egypt, could never for a moment suppose, that after death the soul of a rational being would pass into a beast; that that fair mind, which had told the number of the stars, and penetrated all the dark profundities of nature, was one day to grovel in a grasshopper, or to shine darkling in some glow-worm, as if in emulation of its decayed glories. No; Pythagoras well knew that the soul of man approached too near its Maker ever to fall so low from its splendid exaltation. Pythagoras learned this doctrine in Egypt; and all the world is witness how the Egyptians concealed the most imposing doctrines under the cloak of fables. Could the Magi of Persia, and the Chaldeans, among whom this doctrine originated, according to some- could they, who believed the soul of man to be part of the Deity, could they destine that soul to such deep degradation? They might- there is a possibility that they might; but how small, how minute that possibility! Just like a stone thrown up into the air; there is one solitary possibility that it may never return; but probability and nature are against that possibility.

It is necessary, then, to seek for some elucidation of this

doctrine, which shall exhibit it in a light agreeable to the recognized ideas of the oriental and occidental priesthood. The vulgar notion of metempsychosis has been shewn to be inconsistent with the religions of the priests, by whom it was professed; it is there- fore more than probable, that by the metempsychosis of Pythagoras and the Druids was meant those successive changes through which the human body passes. Firsts it existed as a germ, when the first man drew his breath; a variety of changes ensued till that germ put on the spermatic form; it existed like a vegetable, devoid of feeling, without animation. A third succession of changes brought it into a fetal state, in which it lived like an animal; this change was perfected by birth; and, time elapsing, it changed into another, as reason began to dawn; then, and not before then, man became a living soul. For a short period of years the body serves as a habitation for this soul; but "there is a time, in which it is appointed unto man to die," the body decays, the clay building returns to the dust of the earth, while the soul experiences a new change. It does not die, nor does it sleep; but, clad in a fresh body, fairer than that, which it has left, it experiences new pleasures and sweeter delights. A future resurrection ensues, and, a fresh change is the consequence; but the body, that is now put on, is not what it once was; we shall be changed, this mortal will put on immortality, this corruptible incorruption. Pleasures, which at present it is not, given for us to conceive, will then brighten the fair landscape of enjoyment will all but overwhelm the rising spirit with delight; and, if we may believe the enchanting doctrine of the Oriental sages, another change will complete the heights of bliss, to which we shall attain. This new body will be given to the dust, from whence it came, but the spirit will return to God.

If this be allowed, as the true explanation of the fable of the transmigration of souls, how beautifully and explicitly does it agree with the concomitant circumstances, fabled by the ancients to attend metempsychosis!

Souls that by fate
Are doom'd to take new shapes, at Lethe's brink
Quaff draughts secure, and long oblivion drink.

-Virgil

Lethe was a river, of which it was fabled that souls about to enter new bodies were compelled to drink: its placid surface resembled oil. So soon as the waters had touched their lips, that instant they forgot all their past experience, whether good or bad; no remembrance remained of the state in which they last existed. And is it not so with man? he forgets the state in which he last existed. There is, indeed, a Lethe, a flood of oblivion, of which we all drink, on our entrance into a better change; none can remember the circumstances of his last life, and it is but in prospect that he can anticipate the next.

If this elucidation be correct, we are aware that the Israelites must have believed it, as they looked for future resurrection. But allowing that it is not, and, that the Druids believed that the soul of man can become the soul of a beast, though it is unfair to put that construction on Caesar's words; yet we may perhaps be able to find traces of this belief among the Jews. For instance, they thought that the soul of Elias had transmigrated into the body of our Savior. Josephus expressly states, that the Pharisees believed this doctrine. But it may be said, that the corrupted Jews borrowed this foolish doctrine from their Gentile neighbors in later times; and, to prove that their fathers believed in it, it is necessary to find it in the Mosaic writings. But, it is candidly confessed that no such doctrine is to be found in the Pentateuch, nor even the slighted allusion to it. Yet this is no reason whatever that the Israelites were unacquainted with it. No one would ever deny that the descendants of Abraham believed the immortality of the soul; yet Moses never made the most distant allusion to it when he gave the Israelites their dispensation. Moses never mentions the doctrine of resurrection, he never taught a belief of future judgment, nor does his creed exhibit any thing relating to rewards and punishments, or to a life to come. Yet who would be so rash as to declare that the Jews were entirely ignorant of these points The case is exactly the same with the doctrine of the metempsychosis. Moses, indeed, never discourses of it; yet who would say that they knew nothing about it, after they had lived four hundred years among the Egyptians, with whom this doctrine was especially cultivated? The Chaldeans had a firm belief in transmigration, yet Daniel the prophet became president of one of their colleges; he, therefore, must have been acquainted with, and could not disapprove of it. The circumstance of Daniel becoming president of a college of Chaldeans, considering his belief as a Jew and his attainments as a man of learning, is highly favorable to the construction just put upon this doctrine of transmigration.

Every religion which has been instituted since the floods has had its sacrifices; both the Israelitish and Druidical abounded in these rites. It is, therefore, out part to examine these, and discover what identities may occur. Human sacrifice was offered by the ancient Jews, as many passages in the sacred writings attest. From Leviticus we learn, that if the daughter of any priest degraded her father by the commission of certain sins, she was to be burnt with fire. Jephtha the Gileadite, and judge of Israel, vowed a vow unto the Lord, that he would give him as a sacrifice the first human being, with whom he should meet, and actually offered up his own daughter for a burnt-offering. Upon the capture of Jericho, Joshua, the general of Israel, said concerning the place, that whosoever built it up again, should lay the foundation in his first-born, and in his youngest son should he set up the gates; that is, he should offer them up at such occurrences as an offering to the Almighty. The Levite (mentioned in Judges, xix.) took a knife, and cut his concubine into twelve pieces. In Joshua vii. any man taken with an accursed thing, was to be burnt with fire, a sacrifice to the Lord. Joshua built an altar unto the Lord in Mount Ebal, and hanged the king of Ai on a tree. Samuel too, the prophet of the

Almighty, hewed Agag, king of the Amalekites, in pieces before the Lord, in the temple at Gilgal, which has been spoken of before. If these examples were not sufficient to shew that the Jews were given to this sacrifice so abominable in the eyes of Christians, yet the manner in which they invaded Canaan, and the reason they gave for their massacres, would amply declare, in letters of blood, the fact of their offering human sacrifice. How many thousands of these unsuspecting people did they slay in execution of their commission from the Almighty, "who delighteth not in blood, neither taketh pleasure in the death of the sinner." Concerning their divine command, nothing more need be said; but, the fact that they did make one grand sacrifice of whole nations, avenging the wrath of the Deity upon them, is too well authenticated ever to be denied, and demonstrates how impressed they were with the notion, that the Almighty required human blood to satisfy his awful vengeance.

The immolation of men, and offering of human sacrifice, was prevalent among the Druids. Caesar says, that "they offer men in sacrifice to the gods, for the recovery of the sick" etc. thinking that nothing will appease the immortal gods for the life of man, but the life of man. And he adds that in general they were offered as burnt-offerings. Other writers, ancient and modern, have corroborated this testimony of Caesar's, and many have described the manner in which these rites were performed.

By the Levitical law it was ordained that sheep and oxen should be offered to the Lord. (Lev. xxvii. 26; Num. vii. 87, 88.) Balaam, when besought by Balak, offered a bull and a ram; and, in a vast variety of instances, which might be quoted, the ancient Jews offered these animals in sacrifice. But why bulls and rains, more than any other animals? Why were their sacrificial altars to be adorned with horns? For the same reason that among Gentile nations' altars were sometimes entirely built with horns; and had, in every instance, horns upon some part of them. This was a relic of Tauric worship, which had so universally spread. Else, why was the life of a man considered sacred, when he took refuge between the horns of an altar? There must have been some mystic sanctity attached to bulls and rams, which can only be explained by supposing it to have originated with their ancient worship.

Dr. Borlase; speaking of the Druids, says that they sacrificed sheep and bulls to the Deity. In the temples there is generally a hole through the stone that forms the altar; to this stone the cattle were fastened before they were sacrificed, a rope being passed through it. Whenever the ground around any of these temples is excavated, considerable remains of the bones both of sheep and of oxen are found.

Such are the principal features of the ancient Israelitish worship, and in every point they agree with the Druidical. The same rites, the same ceremonies, the same feasts, the same God, and, in fine, the same religion. If the comparison were carried still further, the- identity would become still more striking. The Israelites looked for a Redeemer who should come m future times; they typified his advent by the scapegoat, and a variety of emblems. The Druids did the same; they looked for some one, who was typified under the emblem of the mistletoe. "The Druids hold nothing more sacred than the mistletoe, and the tree on which it is produced, provided it be the oak. They make choice of groves of oak on this account; nor do they perform any of their sacred rites, without the leaves of these trees; so that one might suppose that they are called for this reason by a Greek etymology, Druids. And, whatever mistletoe grows on the oak, they think is sent from heaven, and is a sign that the Deity has chosen that tree. They very seldom find this, but when they do, they treat it with great pomp. They call it by a name which means the curer of all ills; and, having prepared their feasts and sacrifices under, a tree, they bring to it two white bulk, whose horns are tied. The priest, dressed in white, then ascends the tree, and, with a golden pruning-hook, cuts off the plant, which is caught, ere it touches the ground, in a sheet." (Pliny, Nat. Hist.) Virgil, speaking of the mistletoe, calls it the golden branch, and says, by its efficacious powers alone man could return from the dreary realms beneath. It has already been stated that the Druids adored the Almighty under the representation of the oak, supposing that that tree exhibited in the liveliest manner the God of vegetative nature, eternal, omnipotent, and self-existing, defying the assaults of a past eternity, and looking on the future as only equal to himself in duration. From him came the branch, so much spoken of by ancient prophets, the curer of all our ills, who is indeed "the resurrection and the life," without whose kind assistance we cannot return from the gloomy territories of the grave.

A thousand different cases might be shewn in which these distant people believed alike; but these perhaps will suffice to establish the point of the identity of their religions. An examination of their priestly establishment, will exhibit this in a still clearer light.

Among the Jewish priests there was one, who possessed supreme authority over the rest, who was commonly called the high priest, and answered in every particular to the arch Druid of Britain. Every temple had one or more priests, but the metropolitan temple belonged exclusively to the high priest. So Samuel the prophet was priest at Gilgal; there he crowned kings, and performed the solemnities required by the Jewish ritual. The vestment worn by the high priest of the Jews coincides strikingly with the decorations of the arch Druid. The sacred robes of both were, a linen bonnet, coat, girdle, and breeches; but on the grand day of expiation, the Hebrew priest wore a dress consisting of an embroidered coat of fine linen, a suit of breeches, and a girdle to fasten his garments around. Over this hung another robe, which reached his feet, and on that, the ephod, with the breast-plate of judgment; exactly in the same manner as the British Druid put on his bosom the famous *iodha moran* (breast-plate of judgment), which is still in existence. The dress pf the Jewish high priest bears a very great resemblance to that of our modern Highlanders;

and coincides, in a very striking. manner with that of Abaris, the Hyperborean Druid, as described by Himerius.

The Hebrew hierarchy may be divided into three classes; their priests or judges; their prophet; and, their scribes, doctors or lawyers. Sometimes the two former were joined in, one, but the more common custom was, that they were separate. Just so it was with the Druids; they were divided into three glasses, Druids, vaids, and bards. the Druids were their priests and judges; the vaids were their diviners and physicians; the bards were their poets, heralds, and scribes. If the different offices and occupations of these men were compared, the result would prove how nearly they and their religion were allied to the Jews. The Druids are, perhaps, now extinct; but vestiges are yet left of the vaids and bards, though in the course of a few years they will, in all probability, follow the course which the former have trod. Every day the number of our divining gypsies, and heraldic ballad-singers, seems to decrease. From the summit of grandeur and priestly magnificence these ancient relics have gradually been sinking. In the remembrance of our fathers, every village had its wise man, who governed the joyous sports of the spring, who presided at the May-day festival, and who told the wondering maidens and youth events which were to happen in their future life. In our times each day appears to decrease the number of these people; perhaps our children will not know that they ever existed. Already the May-pole festival begins to decline, the festivities of the first of April are confined to the boarding-school. In many places salutary laws have made proclamation against bon-fires, once lighted in honor of Moloch and Baal. Every remain of druidical religion and learning appears to be fast dying away. *Once*, but it was in times now buried with the past, this religion and this learning enlightened the world with its benign influences, its sun of glory reached its dazzling meridian; now it sets encircled with clouds and blackness shorn of its beauteous beams, and leaving the world in obscurity and night.

RELIGIONS CALLED DRUIDICAL AND HEBREW

The mensuration of time by a night and a day was common both to Hebrews and Britons, and was plainly of antediluvian origin. "God called the light day, and the darkness called he night; and the evening and the forming were the first day." So the first day, which our earth ever saw, was measured in this manner. The Jews, in after times, were commanded to keep their sabbath from even to even. Leviticus, xxxiii. 32. The Druids did the same, as Caesar says, '"Galli se omnes, ab Dite patre prognatos praedicunt, idque ab Druidibus proditum dicunt. Ob eam causam, spatia omnis temporis non numero dierum, sed noctium finiunt, dies natalis et mensium et annorum initia, sic observant ut noctem dies sub-sequatur." Mr. Davies has shewn, that from this very circumstance the fable of the Cimmerian darkness, may be explained, and, the Oriental origin of the Druids proved.

The burial of the dead prevailed among both Druids and Hebrews, with one remarkable circumstance differing from the modern manner of burial, yet common to them. They never buried in coffins, except when they embalmed; the bodies were arrayed in funereal clothes. The manner, in which the modem Jews perform these rites, bears every mark of primeval simplicity, and resembles extremely that of the ancient Egyptians. After invoking the Deity in behalf of the person deceased, they offer up prayer to him, entreating that he will raise up the dead at some future day. Then, an oration being made in praise of the person about to be buried, they, walking round the grave, repeat a prayer for the spirit of the dead; the corpse is then laid in the tomb "in peace." All present put earth on the coffin, and, then, walking backwards, they leave the tomb, throwing blades of grass or flowers on it, and saying, "Thou shalt flourish again, like the grass of the earth." (See Notes to *Rameses*) The Egyptian method was this: "When those who had the care of the dead proceed to embalm the corpse of any person of respectable rank, they first take out the contents of the belly, and place them in a separate Vessel. After the other rites for the dead have been performed, one of the embalmers, laying his hand on the vessel, addressing the Sun, utters, on behalf of the deceased, the following prayer, which Euphantus has translated from the original language, into the Greek: 'Oh thou Sun, our lord, and all ye gods, who are the givers of life to men, accept me, and receive me into the mansions of the eternal gods; for I have worshiped piously, while I have lived in this world, those divinities, whom my parts taught me to adore; I have ever honored those parents, who gave origin to my body; and, of other men, I have neither killed any, nor robbed them of their treasure, nor inflicted upon them any grievous evil: but, if I have done any thing injurious to my own life, either by eating or drinking any thing unlawfully, this offense has not been committed by me, but, by what is contained in this chest;' meaning the intestines in the vessel, which are then thrown into the river. The body is afterwards regarded as pure, this apology having been made for its offenses; and the embalmer prepares it according to the appointed rite." (See Pritchard's Analysis.) The same distinction, between the body and the spirit, was made by the ancient, and still exists among the modem, Jews.

These, then, are a small part of the arguments, which may be brought to evince the identity of the Israelite and Druidical belief. After reading these, can any doubt reasonably remain, in the mind of the most cautions, of the unity of these religions? Two nations, at a great distance from each other, and, having no communication, adore a Being, to whom they ascribe the same attributes, and make him, as has been shewn, the same God. This was the foundation of their modes of worship: they both adored him. in the murky gloom of primeval woods, with the same intentions, and with the same rites. Having the same ideas of his attributes, they both worship; him under the similitude of an oak. In temples- exactly alike, uncovered, and without walls, they cultivated his worship. Each raised up, in thanks, fed gratitude to their Maker, a monumental stone, and made fires to his honor on the top of the cairn. Bel and Moloch are alike adored by both. Both are given to serpent worship; and, both celebrate the kindness of their Maker for the blessings of springs with the same festivities, on the same day of the year, and instituted at one epoch. Telesms, penates, and lares, are found among both; both believe in transmigration; both offer the same sacrifices, whether human or animal, as burnt offerings. Their hierarchy or priesthood are alike; they measure their time in the same manner; their feasts coincide, and are celebrated with the same festivities and rites; they both bury their dead« In. a word, in whatever point we regard the Jewish religion in that the Druidical is found to represent it.

If the adoration of the Divine Being were to be celebrated with different rites by different people, their religion, to use the word in its common acceptation, would be different; for, difference in religion does not so much consist in the different conception of the nature of the Deity, but, in the different rites, ceremonies, etc. used in the performance of his adoration. Here both parties adore the same God, and the rites of one are the same as the rites of the other; and therefore the identity of both is proved.

Perhaps it might be objected that the Almighty is expressly said by sacred writers to have given to his servant Abraham a method of worship perfectly pure, and, to have enlarged that method when his family increased, after, their exit from Egypt; therefore he must have invented (if the phrase can be used) all the different feasts and ceremonies, which he gave with such magnificence from Mount Sinai, and, which, until that time, must have been unknown to man; so that all the calculations concerning Tauric worship, the reasonings about the rise of the Jewish festivals, must be incorrect. This, perhaps, depends on a misconception of the case. When the Almighty gave from the heights of Sinai the Mosaic dispensation, he did not do so with the intent either of contradicting or overturning the patriarchal, except in cases where the former ceremonies had been abused and prostituted to the service of idolatry; therefore, the festivals, which had been celebrated in patriarchal times were not discontinued, but, were given afresh in commemoration of new circumstances. So the feast of Tabernacles was given in commemoration of the Israelites' sojourning forty years in tents, during their passage through the wilderness; but no one would ever deny that this same feast did not exist ages before the Israelites went down into Egypt. Among the Romans it was celebrated in honor of Anna Perenna; and, indeed, prevailed almost all over the world as a Bacchic festival. The Jewish feast of Tabernacles was merely the Tauric feast to Moloch, the Sun, with this alteration, that whereas the Tauric festival was held on the fifteenth day of the eighth month, the feast of tabernacles was hastened by one month, and commenced on the fifteenth of the seventh. The case is exactly the same with the feast of Pentecost, which was the feast of harvest, but, was given to the Jews as a sign that they should commemorate the giving of the law. This custom, indeed, was far from being uncommon in ancient times. So, the Almighty gave to Noah the rainbow, as a sign that the earth should be drowned with water no more; not that the rainbow never existed before, which was an absolute impossibility, but that it was them, for the first time, exhibited as a token to man.

Such are the numerous and striking internal coincidences between these ancient religions. We will now proceed to examine their external relations, which will add additional testimony to the truth of what has been stated. Indeed, by a review of the foreign connections of both Jews and Druids, much more explicit and clearer light may be obtained to shew in what manner both religions were derived from one original, whose relict are to be found all over the world.

The inhabitants of the nations surrounding Judea, with whom the Israelites more particularly had communication, held several opinions in common with them; and it is our business to inquire into each of these opinions severally, and shew that they likewise existed among the nations surrounding Britain, the grand seat of the Druids; thereby proving what is requisite in a more explicit manner than has, hitherto, been done.

The Egyptians believed in a deity, of whom it was said "I am all that has been, is, or shall be." This Deity was called Isis; but their supreme God was Ptha or Cneph, or Agathos daemon, to whom they ascribed every attribute, of a great and magnificent nature. They, too, like the Druids and Israelites, raised up altars to the Deity, as acknowledgments for benefits received from him, and, as solemn attestations of the truth of oaths that they swore by. This practice will be shewn hereafter to have been prevalent over almost all the world. In proof that the Egyptians were given to swearing by their altars, or by the eternal stability and power of the Deity, which was thereby understood, it may merely be stated, that the character in the hieroglyphics, or sacred language, for stability and firm endurance was an altar; and, it may be observed, that the Chinese character wan-tang for the same word, has very much of the same appearance, though this by no means should lead to the opinion that the Chinese character and the Egyptian hieroglyphic are in anywise similar; for, out of all the Egyptian sacred letters, whose meaning has hitherto been discovered, not above half a dozen bear the slightest similitude to the same word in Chinese. The sumptuous temples of the Egyptians shew that they fell very early from the pure theism of the Druids, though many Druidical rites, no doubt, were retained among them. Accordingly, sacred history tells, that very soon after the times of Abraham, who had been an ignicolist, the kings of Egypt knew not the Lord. There cannot be much doubt, that the pyramids, of which we have heard so much, and written so much, are remains of the worship of Bel or Moloch, and were originally cairns, on whose top, fires were lighted in honor of the Sun. It appears that they stand on the solid rock, and exactly answer to the situation of the British cairns. That the Egyptians did worship the Sun, is plain from the adoration of Ammon- or Am-ouein, as Jablonski makes it- who was represented with lines proceeding from his head, in the shape of rays, the word meaning the beneficent effects of the equatorial Sun. Macrobius says, that the Egyptians worshiped the

Sun as the soul of the world, and represented him under various forms according to his different appearances. The serpent was sacred among them; from a variety of concurrent circumstances, it appears that this reptile represented the eternal existence of the Deity, or Eternity, as an hieroglyphic. At the temple of Isis, at Dendera, there is a representation of a procession of men and women, bringing to Isis, and Osiris, who sits behind her, globes surrounded with bulls' horns, mitred snakes, cynocephali, vases, lotus flowers, little boats, graduated staves, and sphinxes. A circle placed on the back of a serpent denotes life; we have already stated that the grand Druidical temple at Abury was of this form, and sacred to the eternal God; perhaps with the assistance of the knowledge of this hieroglyphic, it may be easy to shew that it was dedicated to Baal-zebub, that is, the Lord of life, the soul of the world; indeed, it was not uncommon for the ancients to build their temples in the shape of some hieroglyphic; so the grand temples in India, and the cathedral of Saint Paul's in England, etc. are built in the form of crosses; not that they have the slightest allusion to the cross of Calvary, but that it has been a practice time immemorial, to build temples, pagodas, etc. in the form of crosses. The crux ansata of the Egyptians, (The cross as an Egyptian hieroglyphic, represents the universe, as foil of life and motion.) which Isis always holds in her hand, as may be seen in the statues of her at the British Museum, was the hieroglyphic of life. And, it is said, that, when the Christians were about to destroy the Serapeum in Egypt, the priests told them, in order to appease them, that it represented future life in another world. A serpent joined to the cross alludes to the immortality of the soul; and a serpentine or spiral line represents the mystic number one hundred. Numerous other instances might be mentioned in which the Egyptians held the serpent as a sacred animal; but these perhaps will suffice.

Tauric worship, too, was much cultivated among them. Apis, as every one knows, was represented by a bull; and the globes encircled with bulls' horns, sufficiently attest the origin of this worship, which was celebrated all over the world with dancing, exactly as it was in Britain. "The Egyptians dance round their idols, bowing towards the rising Sun." A bull with a man's arm beneath its feet, holding the branch of a tree full of leaves, is the hieroglyphic of mighty; and, has evident allusion to the mighty influences of Taurus, in causing the vegetative powers of nature, to operate and to furnish man with sustenance and food. Bulls were sacred to Osiris, the Sun; they even carried their Tauric adoration so far as to embalm deceased bullocks, and placed their mummies in splendid sarcophagi, one of which may be seen in the British Museum. The Egyptian priests were great magicians, as appears from sacred writ; for we there find, that they by their incantations even dared to rival Moses, the messenger of the Almighty; and the fact of their having teraphim or telesms, is apparent from the number of lares or household gods still in existence, which once were worshiped by them. They were firm believers in the doctrine of metempsychosis, as is attested by Herodotus, Diogenes Laertius, and Hecataeus; but, in all probability, it was qualified in the manner before mentioned; for, we have already seen that they believed in future life, resurrection, and an hereafter. Diodorus Siculus reports, that they believed the souls of good men went after deaths into an unknown and invisible world.

As to their sacrifices, they offered both human and animal, just as the Jews and Druids did. They offered up men on the tomb of Osiris, at Celeopolis. It is said that they used to sacrifice, once a year, a beautiful young virgin to the river Nile; and, travelers state, that this practice still continues, but, in a less bloody manner, as they offer in the stead of beauty and youth, only an image of clay. In almost every respect the ancient Egyptian priests are similar to the Bonzes of India, China, and Japan, who, like them, offer human sacrifices, believe in rewards and punishments, keep Tauric festivals, adore serpents, and look for a world to come. The scarabaeus, or beetle, forms one of the principal figures under which these people adored vegetative nature. Indeed, in some of their zodiacs the scarabaeus occupies the place of Cancer; and, from the frequency of its introduction among their hieroglyphics, the sacred esteem, in which it was held may be surmised. The sphinx was a representation of the signs Leo and Virgo joined together, in commemoration of the inundation of the Nile, which occurred when the Sun was in those signs. They had always a sort of astronomical mystic reverence for the three signs Cancer, Leo, Virgo.

There is a curious circumstance, which, perhaps, it is worthwhile noticing, concerning the Sphinx worship, viz. that it must have originated much about the same time as the Tauric worship; for the Nile ceases to overflow its banks towards the latter end of August, or beginning of September. Now, it is evident, that, when the Sun entered Taurus on the first day of May, he entered Leo and Virgo in August and September respectively: hence the origin of the worship of the sphinx, and the period of its institution. That there existed a great similarity between the theology of Egypt, and, that of the Druids and Israelites, is attested still more powerfully by two very curious circumstances. It is well known, that in Egypt there are magnificent ruins of temples, fragments of pillars, huge blocks of stone, and amazing masses of granite at a place called *Karnac*. In France, at a place called Camac, the same sort of monuments, in the same situation, and the same state, exist. Upon this strange coincidence no comment is required.

"Herodotus (see Toland's Druids) says, in the second book of his History, that, near to the entrance of the magnificent temple of Minerva, at Sais, in Egypt, of which he speaks with admiration, he saw an edifice 21 cubits in length, 14 in breadth, and 8 in height, the whole consisting only of one stone; and that it was brought thither by sea, from a place about twenty days' sailing from Sais. This is my first instance, and, parallel to it, all those who have been at Hoy, one of the Orkneys, do affirm, without citing, or many of them without knowing, this passage in Herodotus, that there lies on a barren heath in this island, an oblong stone, in a valley between two hills, called, I suppose antiphrastically, or by way of contraries, the dwarfy stone. It is 36 feet long, 18 feet broad, and 9 feet high. No other stones are near it. 'Tis all hollowed within, or, as we may say, scooped by human art and industry, having a door on the east side, two feet square, with a stone of the same dimensions, about two feet from it, which was intended, no doubt, to close the entrance. Within, at the south end of it, cut out in the form of a bed and pillow, capable to hold two persons, as at the north end there is another bed- Dr. Wallace says a couch- both very neatly done. Above, at an equal distance from both, is a large round hole, which is supposed not only designed for letting in the light and air, but likewise for letting out of smoke from the fire, for which there is a place, in the middle between the two beds. The marks of the workman's tool appear everywhere." Upon this I shall remark as upon the last, that no comment whatever is required.

It is quite plain, that Joseph and the Egyptians, see Gen. xl. 8, had the same God; and again, in Gen. xli., as Pharaoh himself confessed it in verse 38 of the same chapter. But, at that time they were fast falling from the true religion; for, when the sons of Jacob went down into Egypt, but a few years afterwards, to buy bread, Joseph found it necessary to inform them that he himself feared the true God. But from the first chapter, of Exodus, it appears, that they, in a very few years after, neither knew Joseph nor his God. Such are the proofs which may be urged in defense of the opinion that the religion of the Israelites, Egyptians, and Druids, were once alike. (It may be here remarked, without being very irrelevant to the text, that the Egyptian hieroglyphics bear a great resemblance to those of the Greeks.)

In Canaan there appears to have been no temples before the Israelitish invasion. When the patriarch Abraham sojourned there, the religion and language of the country were similar to his own. But, like to their neighbors the Egyptians, in the time of Moses, they were complete idolaters, and knew nothing about the true God. From adoring the Divine Being under the solar emblem,

they began to adore the Sun himself as a God. It appears from the
Pentateuch, that they worshiped Moloch in exactly the same
manner as the Druids, leaping through the fires which they lighted
in his honor. Bel, was another especial object of their adoration:
indeed, they worshiped the San under a complete variety of names
Bel, Moloch, Ourchad, Adonis, Tammuz; of the last, Milton says,
Paradise Lost, book i. 446:

> Tammuz came next behind,
> Whose annual wound in Lebanon allured
> The Syrian damsels to lament his fate,
> In amorous ditties, all a summer's day;
> While smooth Adonis, from his native rock,
> Ran purple to the sea, supposed with blood
> Of Tammuz yearly wounded; the lore-tale
> Infected Zion's daughters with like heat.

These mournful ditties for Tammuz or Adonis were
forbidden by the prophets to the Israelites, which shews, that they
were but too much inclined to perform them. The festival of
Adonis was celebrated at the commencement of autumn at the
same time as that of Moloch: in other countries, its signification is
too apparent to be mistaken. Plutarch says, that Adonis, Tammuz,
Bacchus, Osiris, were all one Deity; and there is no doubt but that
they all represented the Sun. The feasts of Tammuz or Adonis
occurred twice in a year; once as mentioned above, and, again, at
the commencement of spring; and, therefore it originated at the
same time as the Tauric worship of the Druids and Israelites, to
which it certainly belonged. They welcomed the spring at the
festival of Bel, with dancing and joyous shouts; they mourned the
departure of the Sun in autumn, after his kindness in clothing the
earth with fruits, with weeping and mournful ditties.

Carthage, which was a colony from Canaan, contained a
considerable mass of Druidical remains. Baal was the greatest of
the Carthaginian gods; his temples and altars were on eminences,

upon which large fires were kindled, as on the British cairns. The people danced in wild vehemence round these fires, and, human sacrifices were offered. The Carthaginians were accustomed to swear, like the Druids, by the eternal stability of the Deity; so, the father of Hannibal made him swear on the altar of Bel, eternal hatred to the Romans. From the very composition of many of the Carthaginian, Tyrian, and British proper names, the adoration in which Baal was held by them may be perceived; thus Ahi*bal*, Hanni*bal*, *Bal*timore, etc.

The Americas, when discovered by the Spaniards, had a great many practices among them of a Punic character. Perhaps if proper research was made into their antiquities, their Punic origin would become much more apparent. The Carthaginians had groves among them, as appears from Virgil's Aeneid; so had the Mexicans. It has been reported (Moeurs de Sauvages) that a Huronnite woman, to whom a Christian missionary was describing the attributes of the Almighty God, cried out with amazement, "What is it that I hear? I perceive that the God, you are telling me of, is our Ares-koni;" that is, their supreme Deity. The Incas of Peru, the Emperors of Mexico, and the Chiefs of Chili, all pretend to be descendants of the Sun, to whom they offer human sacrifice, and whom they regard as a God. All over America the people had telesms or teraphim, called by them Man-i-tou. Both Carthaginians and Americans believed in transmigration.

With regard to the Persians, Pliny remarked the affinity of their religion, to that of the Druids: he says: "The Britons know so much as to be able to instruct even the Persians;" which sentence alone is sufficient to prove the great similarity of the two, if, even, it were not borne out by other demonstrative arguments. The Persians in general have been charged as ignicolists, or adorers of fire. They kept a sacred fire constantly burning in honor of Mithras, the Sun, who had neither temple nor image, for the very same reason that he had not in Britain; Herodotus says, because they thought it ridiculous to attempt to enclose the Deity in walls, or represent him under a graven form. In this worship of fire they were not at all singular; Abraham, the great progenitor of the Jews, according to Eastern accounts, was an ignicolist, and dwelt at Ur, of the Chaldeans, (Ur means *fire* or light; the city probably had its name from the pyropic worship there cultivated.) until called into other lands by the Deity. Anciently the Almighty was supposed to appear, most frequently, as a flame of fire; so Moses saw him under that appearance when he blazed in the incombustible bush. The Lord appeared in fire on Mount Sinai. Moses himself taught, that the Deity was a consuming fire. (Deut. iv. 24.) In accordance with this idea, he instituted that "the fire should ever be burning upon the altar, it should never go out" (Lev. vi. 13); which institute was exactly the same as that of the ancient Persians, from whom the Jews had received it, through the hands of die patriarch Abraham, whose father, Terah, as expressly stated by Scripture, was an idolater. In the whole of their history they never appear to have had any objection to the worship of fire. Jacob married two idolatrous wives- Moses married the daughter of an idolater, etc. That this worship was extremely prevalent among the Persians, there cannot be any doubt; the whole province of Media was called *azarbigan*, by them, from an old Persic word *azar*, which means fire. Pyrolatry seems at one time to have been prevalent all over the face of the earth. Huet says, that it was celebrated in the same manner as the orgies of Bacchus, at the feast of Mithras, and is to be found among the Jews, Chaldeans, Phrygians, Lycians, Medes, Scythians, Sarmatian, in Pontus, Cappadocia, India, Arabia, Egypt, Ethiopia, Libya: it existed in the worship of Jupiter Ammon, and among the Garamantea, with the vestals, who were appointed to guard it. Every town in Greece had a pyrtanon; Hercules was worshiped in Gaul under this emblem; Vulcan on Etna, and Venus Ericyna; and in Ireland, England, Muscovy, Tartary, China, America, Mexico, Peru, and many other places, it is to be found.

It has been already stated, that this worship was instituted in honor of Mithras, the Sun, to whom human sacrifices were offered, which cruel custom Commodus the Roman emperor abolished. They had a festival on the day when that luminary entered the sign Taurus, which was celebrated by them in much the same manner as that in Britain. Several authors declare, that the Mithraitic mysteries were similar to those of Isis in Egypt, and Ceres at Eleusis. This Mithras was likewise adored by them in groves and high places, where he passed under the same denomination as in Britain, Bel, which name they frequently joined to their, proper appellations as Mahabel, (a monarch of the Mahabadian dynasty), in a very similar manner to the British and Carthaginians. Their ignicolistic, or Phoebean worship, was in honor of the Sun, who was, in their view, the most majestic type of the Almighty. That they did not worship fire itself, is plain from the words of Ferdausi, who says, according to Sir W. Jones, "Think not that they were adorers of fire; for that element was only an exalted object, on the luster of which they fixed their eyes. They humbled themselves a whole week before God; and, if thy understanding be ever so little exerted, thou must acknowledge thy dependence on a Being supremely pure." The Persians appear to have been acquainted primarily with the purest of all religions. "A firm belief that one supreme God made the world by his power, and, continually governed it by his providence; a pious fear, love, and adoration of him; a due reverence for parents and aged persons; a fraternal affection for the whole human species; and, a compassionate tenderness even for. the brute creation." Such was the religion of the first Persians; the beauties of which, as far surpass both the patriarchal and Mosaic, as the blazing splendor, of the noon-day sun shine dazzling beyond the submissive rays of the silver moon: in fact, it is nothing less than Christianity, extended, even, to the brute creation.

It may not here be amiss to exhibit, a slight difference between the Persic, Druidic, and Judaic religions, and to explain bow that difference; arose. When that pure religion, just referred to, ceased to exist in Persia, and, when the god, who was the object of it, began to be worshiped under similitudes, the

Mithraitic, Belie, or Sabean religions succeeced, and pyrolatry commenced. It was at this-time that Abram was called by the Deity, from out of the land of the Chaldeans, where he had been a Sabean priest, as the sacred writings inform us, though it does not appear why he left his brethren, the Chaldeans. No doubt, some dispute had arisen concerning the method of worship, in which, though differing, perhaps, but in very minute circumstances from the received faith, he was opposed by the priesthood unanimously, and forced to fly away, with no adherents but his own family, among whom alone his method of worship descended. As a mark of divine approval of this circumstance, the Almighty instituted the rite of circumcision, which cannot be found either among Druids or Persians, but which, nevertheless does not affect the general proposition and inquiry.

The coincidence of the Persian and Druidical religion is, still more strikingly, illustrated by the similarity of the Persepolitan arrow-headed characters, and by the Druidical Ogham mysterious writing. On a stone in the British Museum, taken from the ruins of Persepolis, is this inscription;

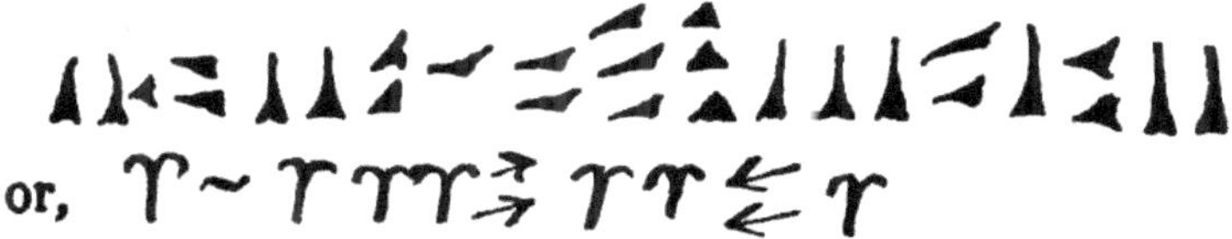

And the following is a specimen of the Ogham (virgular):

Iran is the true name for the country, which we, ignorantly, denominate Persia, the latter being merely a province of the former Empire. The oldest languages, supposed by Oriental scholars to have been spoken in Iran, were the Sanskrit and

Chaldaic; and, from them the language of the Zend, the Pahlavi, and the Hebrew sprung- the two latter being derived from the Chaldaic, which will sufficiently account for the fact that Abraham spoke the Hebrew; as to the coincidence of the Druidical Ogham and the Persepolitan arrow-headed letters, it may have been caused by the emigration of the first inhabitants of Britain from Armenia or from the shores of the Caspian Sea, as is attested by almost all British writers. Perhaps, it was in this manner that the religion of the British Druids came to resemble that of the ancient Persians, being but a branch of the original stock, which, as Sir W. Jones states, spread from Iran as from a center, and peopled the world; the emigrating tribes carrying with them the religion, learning, and sciences of the people from whom they sprung.

Arabia contains numerous specimens of Druidic remains; and, the Arabic writings of any antiquity abound with them. The book of Job, which is, on all hands, allowed to have been an Arabic production, has frequent allusions to them. The extraordinary age of this book may be shewn from a consideration of several different circumstances; the length of this patriarch's life was such that he could not have lived at any comparatively modern times. And, again, from chap, xxxviii. 31: "Canst thou bind the sweet influences of Pleiades or loose the bands of Orion?" Where Chimah is used for the Pleiades, and Chesil for Orion. Now, the Pleiades were denominated, by the Romans, Vergiliae, from their formerly rising when spring commenced; and the sweet influences blessed the year by the beginning of spring; by the American Indians Te Jeunoniakoua, that is, the dancers, from the festivities celebrated at their vernal rise; by the Arabs they are denominated Sureea; so where Sureea is used for the Pleiades, and Aiyak for the Hyades by the Persians; and, they are called Chimah again in the book of Job, chap. ix. 9, where Chesil is again used for Orion, When the Pleiades rose at the commencement of spring, Orion rose in the depth of winter; and they were, therefore, the most proper types of spring and winter, that could possibly be invented; their very name carries as much with it; for one term means warmth, and another, cold. From all this it is quite plain that an allusion is made in the text in question, to the Tauric worship; and, therefore, the book of Job must have been written, when Tauric worship had begun to spread.

In accordance with this we find many specimens of Druidic rites in this very ancient book: so in chapter 6, v. 25, etc. which is rendered in our version, "And thou shalt be in league with the stones of the field," evidently, alluding to the same custom, by which Jacob secured himself from the predatory attacks of Laban, by raising up a stone to the Lord; and the Druids in Britain raised up their lithoi. His conceptions of the Almighty are exactly the same as those of the Israelites. He believes in rewards and punishments in a future world, "where the wicked cease from troubling, and the weary are at rest," in angelic influence, resurrection; and, indeed, the whole of his doctrines bear so close a resemblance to those of the Israelites, that modern divines have thought proper to class the poem bearing his name, among the canonical books of sacred writ.

The ancient Arabians admit one supreme God, called Allah Taala, or, the most high God; their religion was pure theism, though they soon fell into the error of adoring the Sun, as Sir W. Jones has stated. Their idol, Manah, was a large upright stone, similar perhaps to the first Jupiter of the Romans. Many of the sects of Arabians believed in transmigration; and, in general their opinions have inclined towards the Pythagorean doctrines. Their festivals were, always, celebrated with dancing and joyous sport- for, they thought that tears and lamentations were disagreeable to the Deity. Upon the whole, however, their theology appears much. purer than that of any of the neighboring nations.

In Babylon the people adored Bel, the Sun; and many of their kings were called after him, as Bel-shazzar. It was, indeed, on the evening of the grand festival to the Sun that this mistress of the world sunk, like Troy, beneath her own flaming ruins. Her king was slain- the kingdom was taken from Belshazzar, and given to Cyrus and the Medes. The temple of Belenus, Belus, or Bel, was once the wonder of the world, rivaling the pyramids of Egypt for antiquity and magnificence. In it there was a statue to the Sun, built of ivory and fragrant wood gilded; this statue was forty feet high, and stood on a pedestal whose elevation was fifty feet. Daniel, the most learned of all the prophets, tells how they burnt people as a punishment; and other authors declare that they offered up human sacrifice to propitiate Moloch. They buried their dead.

The Chaldeans, who were a college of priests connected with the Babylonian empire, have long been celebrated for their amazingly extensive learning. It is said that they took their origin from Zeratusth, though no one can say who Zeratusth was, perhaps, like Thoth of the Egyptians, Hermes of the Greeks, and Mercury of the Romans, he existed but as a personification of science and learning; and, therefore, might well be supposed to be the founder of this learned sect, whose origin was buried in oblivion. The mysteries instituted by this personage, are said to have very much resembled those of Ceres Eleusinia and Isis Egyptiaca. Like them, they were known but to a very few "initiated," and it was only after passing the most terrific ordeal, that any one could be permitted to learn them. Eusebius has stated, that they believed in one supreme lord of life, and giver of good; they likewise had another being, corresponding to the Arimanius of the Persians, the Satan of the Jews, and Devil of the Christian church; though, like both Jews and Christians, he formed no part of their belief. Perhaps they carried their ideal opinions much farther than in modem times. We Christians do not admit a belief of him into our creed. The. Israelites seem to have considered him as an imaginary personage, and to have attributed all, both good and evil, to the Deity. So Isaiah, the Hebrew prophet, says, "I am the Lord, and there is none else. I form the light, and create the darkness; I make peace, and create evil. I the Lord do all these things." They supposed the human soul to be an emanation of the Deity- a notion extremely common in the East; and as ancient as it was common; calculated to fill the soul with the most sublime ideas, and raise it to the most exalted heights of adoration, of which it is capable. High places, or groves, were looked upon by these Chaldeans as the most suitable abodes for religion. They appear to have been the first, who raised temples to their gods, of iron, wood, brass, and stone. They believed in the future changes of the soul, in a manner similar to that described under transmigration. The serpent was sacred among them; and it appears, from Daniel, vi. 7, that the Chaldaic months like that of the Jews and Druids, consisted of thirty days. The ancient Babylonian letters greatly resembled the Persepolitan arrow-headed characters, and the Oghams of Ireland; shewing that, anciently, there was some connection in the learning and language of the East and West, as well as in their religions. The following line, which is taken from a cylindrical brick, was found among the ruins of Babylon:

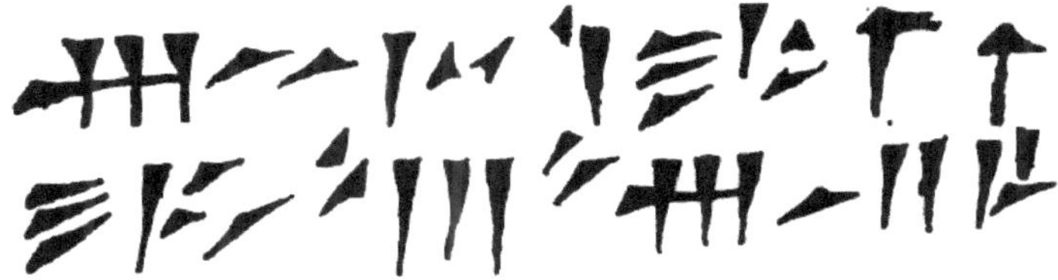

The Ninevitish character resembles in a still nearer manner the Oghamic letters:

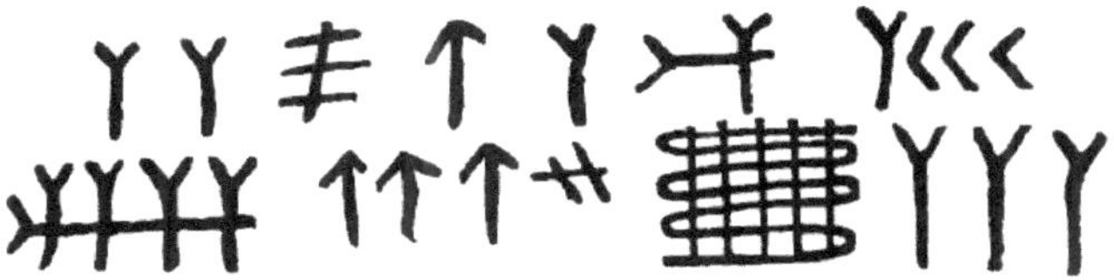

The Gymnosophists, of whom the Greeks spoke so much, and fabled still more, held the same opinions as the Bramins of India, being firm believers both in the immortality of the soul, and its transmigration after death. They celebrated the orgies of Bacchus in the most vehement manner; and adored the Sun, to whom they prayed every morning. The Etruscans, who were the first inhabitants of Italy, coincided in most points of belief with the Gymnosophists, and held similar opinions to the Druids. The Umbrians did the same; and, this is well accounted for by Toland, who proves that they descended from the Gauls or Druids. They adored a trinity of divinities, called by them Cabin, which has been explained by some "Dii potentes" the supreme or chief of them being called Jao, or Javoh. Beneath these Cabiri they placed a host of other lesser deities, personifications, and created things, as the sun, the planets, etc. They were ignicolists, being attached to the Pythagoric system of the world, looking for a future transmigration, and believing in the immortality of the soul. Their Sabean origin is evident, both from their creed and their language, which seems to have been a sister dialect of the Phoenician. The following is an exhibition of an Etruscan alphabet:

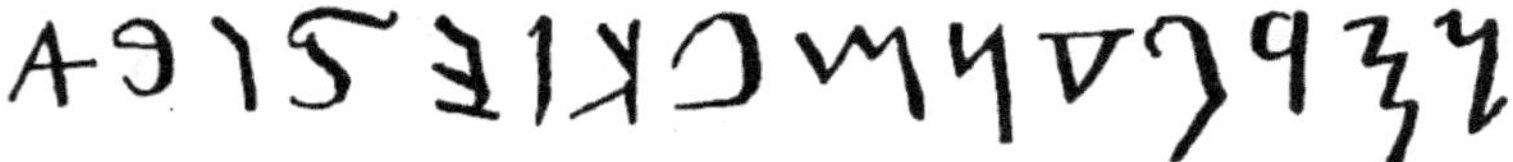

A B G D E I K L M N O P R S T

their corresponding letters in the Phoenician being-

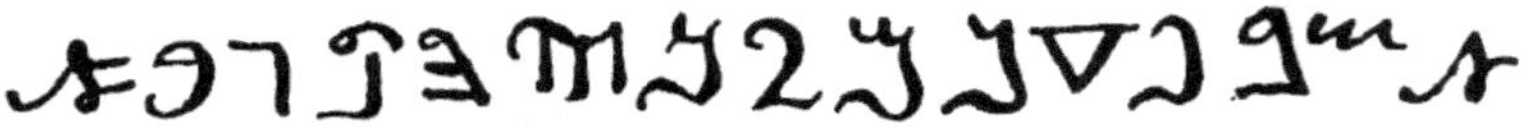

Both these alphabets have a very near relation to the Samaritan, which, perhaps, is one of the most beautiful in the world.

The Druidical religion is very prevalent in India, as has long been remarked by learned men; but there is no relic left of it so striking as that of the Tauric festivals, which still continue in their pristine glory. In a communication from Colonel Pearse to the Asiatic Researches- a work never sufficiently to be praised, and which has thrown more light upon the recondite history of the world, than thousands of other productions- we find the following passage inserted: "I beg leave to point out to the Society, that the Sunday before last was the festival of Bhavani, which is annually celebrated by the Gopaa, and all other Hindus who keep horned cattle, for use or profit. On this feast they visit gardens, erect a pole in the fields, and adorn it with pendants and garlands. The Sunday before last was our first of May, on which the same rites are performed by the same class of people in England, where it is well known to be a relic of ancient superstition in that country. It should seem, therefore, that the religions of the East and the old religion of Britain had a strong affinity. Bhavani has another festival, but that is not kept by any one set of Hindus in particular, and this is appropriated to one class of people. This is constantly held on the ninth of Baisach, which does not always fall on our first of May, as it did this year. Those members of the Society who are acquainted with the rules which regulate the festivals, may be able to give better information concerning this point. I only mean to point out the resemblance of the rites performed here and in England; but must leave abler hands to investigate the matter further, if it should be thought deserving of the trouble. I find that the festival which I have mentioned is one of the most ancient among the Hindus. During the Huli, when mirth and festivity reign among every class, one subject of diversion is to send the people on errands and expeditions that are to end in disappointment, and raise a laugh at the expense of the person sent. The Huli are always in March, and the last day is always the greatest holyday. All the Hindus, who are on that day at Jaggannuth are entitled to certain distinctions, which they hold to be of such importance, that I found it expedient to stay there till the end of the festival; and am of opinion, and so are the rest of the officers, that I saved above five hundred men by the delay. The origin of the Huli seems lost in antiquity, and I have not been able to pick up the smallest account of it."

RELIGIONS CALLED DRUIDICAL AND HEBREW

"If the rites of May-day shew any affinity between the religion of England in times past and that of the Hindus in these times may not the custom of making April-fools on the first of that month, indicate some traces of the Huli? I have not yet heard any account of the origin of the English custom, but it is unquestionably very ancient, and is still kept up, even in great towns, though less in them than in the country. With us it is chiefly confined to the lower classes of people, but in India high and low join in it; and the late Sujaul Daulah, I am told, was very fond of making Huli-fools, though he was a Mussulman of the highest rank. They carry it here so far as to send letters, making appointments in the name of persons, who it is known must be absent from their houses at the time fixed on; and the laugh' is always in proportion to the trouble given."

The following extract from the same volume of the same work is so. very curious, and at, the same time bears so much upon the hinge of this essay, that it is impossible not to quote it at length. It is written by Mr. Reuben Burrow, under the title, "A proof that the Hindus had the Binomial Theorem."

"From the aforesaid country (Tartary) the Hindu religion probably spread over the whole earth; there are signs of it in every northern country, in almost every system of worship. In England it is obvious; Stonehenge is evidently one of the *temples of Boodh*; and the arithmetic, the astronomy, the astrology, the holyday games, names of the stars, and figures of the constellations, ancient monuments, laws, and even the languages of the different nations, have the strongest marks of the same original. The worship of the Sun and fire, human and animal sacrifices, etc. have apparently once been universal; the religious ceremonies of the papists seem in many parts to be a mere servile copy of those of the Goseigns and Fakeers; the Christian ascetics were very little different from their filthy original, the Byraygys, etc. Even the hell of the northern nations is not at all like the hell of the Scriptures, except in some few particulars; but, it is so striking a likeness of the hell of the Hindus, that I should not be surprised if the story of the soldier that saw it in Saint Patrick's purgatory, described in Matthew Paris's history, should hereafter turn out to be a mere translation from the Sanskrit, with the names changed. The different tenets of popery and deism have a great similarity to the two doctrines of Brahma and Boodh; and, as the Bramins were the authors of the Ptolemaic system, so the Boodhists appear to have been the inventors of the ancient Philolaic, or Copernican, as well as the doctrine of attraction; and probably too the established religion of the Greeks and the Eleusinian mysteries, may only be rarities of the two different sects. Thai the Druids of Britain were Bramin, is beyond the least shadow of a doubt; but, that they were all murdered, and their sciences lost, is out of the bounds of probability: it is much more likely that they turned schoolmaster, freemasons and fortune-tellers; and, in this way, part of their sciences might easily descend to posterity, as we find they have done. An old paper, said to have been found by Locke, bears a considerable degree of internal evidence, both of its own antiquity and of this idea; and on this hypothesis it will be easy to account for many difficult matters, that perhaps cannot so clearly be done on any other, and particularly of the great similarity between the Hindu sciences and ours; a comparison between our oldest scientific writers and those of the Hindus, will set the matter beyond dispute; and fortunately the works of Bede carry us twelve hundred years back, which is near enough to the times of the Druids to give hopes of finding there some of their remains. I should have made the comparison myself, but Bede is not an author to be met with in this country; however, I compared an astrolabe, in the Nagry character, (brought by Dr. Mackinnon from Jynagur,) with Chaucer's description, and found them to. agree most minutely; even the center-pin, which Chaucer calls the Horses, has a horse's head upon it in the instrument: therefore, if Chaucer's description should happen to be a translation from Bede, it will be a strong argument in favor of the hypothesis; for we, then, could have nothing from the Arabians."

RELIGIONS CALLED DRUIDICAL AND HEBREW

If any thing more were necessary to exhibit the identity of the priesthood of India and that of Britain, it might be amply supplied by a very slight consideration of the different rite» and customs prevalent among each. They believed that it was a Being perfectly pure and goody who created the universe, who kindly-watched over and governed it by his providence, whose beneficent hand scattered blessings on all his creatures. Yes, it was the Great One, who directed the ponderous planets, in their courses, who gave their enchanting fragrance to the sandal tree and to the rose, who enameled the earth with verdure, and. made it a fit habitation for the peerless majesty of the first of all created beings, man. As God was a spirit, he was inconceivable; as he was invisible, he could not have form; and, from. what was beheld of his works, the conclusion was inevitable, that he was omniscient, omnipotent, omnipresent, and eternal. The universe being his habitation, and himself so pure, so good, yet so tremendously grand (to use the words of an Hindu), "the sun need not shine to illuminate that place, nor the moon, nor the stars; there lightnings need not flash, nor even the fire to burn; for, God irradiates all this bright substance, and, by his effulgence the whole universe beams with glory."

The absorption doctrine, as it has vulgarly been called in Europe, was as common in India as in the rest of the East. A series of transmigrations were commonly reckoned necessary, before the body was absorbed in the Deity. Sheep and bulls were sacrificed. The Cabin, or Dii potentes, were adored in Britain, India, and Greece especially, where their mysteries were celebrated under the well-known title of "Eleusinian Mysteries." This was the concluding phrase of the sacred ceremonies of both east and west, being pure Sanskrit. Warburton has very justly guessed that these, mysteries were instituted for no other purpose than to teach the initiated the true religion, and expose to them the falsity of the idolatrous system promulgated among the people. Cicero seems very much to favor this opinion; when speaking of them he says, "neque solum cum laetita vivendi rationem accepimus, sed etiam cum spe meliori moriendi." It is not in the more modem times of Greece, when under the jurisdiction of the Roman governors, that we are to expect to find traces of Druidic or Israelitish worship; but, in the times of her Homers and Hesiods: then, we discover that the same religion and the same rites were in use among the Greeks as among Egyptians, Persians, Arabians, Babylonians, Chaldeans, Gauls, Etruscans, Hindus, Israelites, and, Druids.

The conceptions of the Deity among the educated in Greece have already been detailed, and their coincidence with those of the Britons already shewn; it only now remains to exhibit a few of the more particular rites and opinions entertained and promulgated among them; and first, the sanctity, in which they held the oak tree. According to their poets, the oak was sacred to Jove; beneath its ample brandies the mystic prophecies of the Deity were half heard, as the passing breezes shook the waving leaves.

"O thou supreme, high throned all height above!
O great Pelasgic, Dodonean Joye!
Who, midst surrounding frosts and vapors dull,
Presid'st on bleak Dodonus, vocal hill;
Whose groves the Selli, race austere, surround;
Their feet unwashed, their slumbers on the ground.
Who hear from rustling oaks thy dark decrees,
And catch the fates low whispered from the breeze-
Hear as of old..."

(The Pelasgi are generally supposed to have been the parent branch of the Etruscans, which plainly accounts for their adoration of the oak.)

Dodona was not the only place in Greece, where oaks and groves were held sacred; numerous instances occur in almost every writer, and the generality of the circumstance is quite evident. The raising up of stones for the same purposes as in

Britain and Judea, appears to have been prevalent in Greece. So, one was raised over the grave of Achilles and Patroclus, which Alexander the Great anointed with oil.

Sarpedon, too, the king of the Lycians, had a stone raised upright over his tomb.

> "His sacred corse bequeath
> To the soft anus of silent sleep and death:
> They to his friends the mournful charge shall bear;
> His friends a tomb and pyramid shall rear:
> What honors mortals after death receive,
> Those unavailing honors let us give."

The doctrine of metempsychosis was so prevalent among the Pythagoric, and other sects in Greece, that several learned men in Europe have supposed Pythagoras to have been its inventor; but that has been shewn to be incorrect. Indeed, the philosophy and religion of Pythagoras so much resembled that of the Druids, that, by most of their contemporary writers, the Druids are expressly declared to have been Pythagoreans. They could not derive their religion and literature from Pythagoras and the Greeks; for, they had attained to a zenith of glory, while the Greeks were yet in a barbarous state. Probably, they were a branch of the priesthood of the ancient Pelasgi, who were the first inhabitants of Greece, and who were the fathers of the Etruscans. Caesar says of the Druids, that though forbidden to write any of their mysteries, yet, when they have occasion to write, they use the Greek letters; which letters must have been nearly similar to the Etruscan, already given, and proves incontestably the near affinity of the Druids and Greeks.

Greek literature has been so long and so ardently studied of late years, that there is but little need of tracing the Druidical rites and creeds. A few extracts from any writer on Greek antiquities will convince the most scrupulous. "The Greeks, like most other nations, worshiped their gods on the summits of high mountains:

> 'Hector, whose zeal whole hecatombs has slain.
> Whose grateful fumes the gods received with joy,
> From *Ida's summits* and the towers of Troy..'

Homer, in his hymn to Apollo, says the top of the highest mountains were sacred to Apollo, or the Sun, The building of round temples is traced to the same source exactly as the Israelitish, from a superstitious reverence paid by the ancients to the memory of deceased friends, relations, etc. and which were first erected only as magnificent monuments in honor of the dead. Nor is it to be wondered that monuments should, in time, be converted into temples; since it was usual at every common sepulcher to offer prayers, etc. It was a common opinion of the Greeks, that the gods alighted in woods or mountains, or by fountains; therefore they built temples in such places; wherever they stood, they faced the rising Sun, they who worshiped standing with their faces: towards the East; this being an ancient custom among the heathen."

"As among, the most ancient Egyptians, the temples were without statues, so the Greeks worshiped their gods without any visible representation, till the time of Cecrops, the founder of Athens. At first the idol was a rude stock, and was, therefore, called so. Such was that of Juno Samia, afterwards converted into a statue." In Achiaia, were thirty square stones, on which were engraved the names of the gods, without any representation. In Delos there was a very ancient statue of Venus, which had a square stone instead of feet. No idols were more common than those of oblong stones erected, and thence termed pillars. These stones, and others of different figures, were generally of a black color, which seems to have been thought the most solemn and appropriate for religious purposes. Even in the most refined ages, these unformed statues were held in mystic reverence for their antiquity. The statues of Jupiter, when luxuriance had taught the Greeks the art of carving, were, generally, made of oak. Before temples were erected, altars were built in groves; the celestial gods were worshiped on the summits of high mountains. The same reason appears to have governed both Druids and Greeks in their grove worship:

> "Lucus Aventino suberat niger ilicis umbra
> Quo possis viso dicere Numen adest.
>
> A darksome grove of oak appeared near,
> Whose gloom impressive told, a God dwells here."

The Greeks used to offer human sacrifice to Bacchus, the Sun, and to the other gods, aft propitiatory. Their priests frequently held the sovereign authority, as Anius, the priest of the Sun, mentioned in Virgil's Aeneid; and Samuel at Gilgal. Indeed the coincidences are so amazingly striking that anyone who reads a treatise on the religion of the belief of the ancient Greeks, must confess their extreme similarity with those of the Druids. (See Robinson's Greek Ant.)

The derivation and origin of all the ancient Roman rites and ceremonies may be found either among the Etruscans, Sabines, or Greeks. This accounts for the customs of the Romans agreeing in so many points with those of the Druids. Eusebius says the Jupiter of the Romans was the same as. Beel or Baal of the Babylonians: he was adored on the top of the Capitoline rock, where the first temple ever built in Rome was erected; and his image was a square block of stone, by which the Romans swore their most tremendous oaths, "Per Jovem lapidem." The oak was sacred to his divinity. The mistletoe was reckoned sacred among them, as Virgil reports in his sixth Aeneid; and lithoi were held in adoration under various names, as, Dii Termini, etc. The circular temples appear to have been frequent in Rome; to this very day the magnificent Pantheon rears its towering summit uncovered and circular, Tauric worship was cultivated among the Romans, as in the celebration of the festivities of Anna Perenna, or Anna Puma Devi, By the laws of the twelve tables, grove worship was expressly enjoined; and, in numerous instances, the Romans pretended to receive prophecies from the gods, goddesses, and nymphs who inhabited them, so, Numa received the doctrines he delivered to the people from the nymph Egeria, in a grove of oak-trees. Human sacrifice was offered by the ancient Romans, to propitiate the vengeance of the gods. The worship of Mithras was imported from Persia, and was joined to that of Apollo, both being personifications of the Sun, as appears from an altar, on which is inscribed "Mithras Deo Soli invicto Mithra."

From all this evidence it appears, that the Druidical faith prevailed, not only in Britain, but, likewise, all over the East, and, more especially, its relics are to be found in Judea. The most natural account that can be given of its great extension and universality, is only on a supposition, that it is a branch of the ancient Zabian religion, which will explain every attendant circumstance most minutely. A series of ages have overcast with dimness and obscurity the rise and origin of this ancient belief, ao that but few monuments remain, by which we can judge what it once was, and compare it with itself in distant lands. But from all the evidence adduced, and all the examples exhibited, its identity with the religion of the forefathers of the Jews, before the Levitical dispensation, can never be doubted. Internal and external proofs press on every side, and he must be a skeptic, indeed, who could doubt their force. Perhaps, at some future period, a larger treatise may shew something of the origin, rise, progress, and ruin of the Zabian faith; but, for the present, all these things seem to be involved in an impenetrable mist. The Druidical religion rose like the Sun, the grand object of its culture, and reached the topmost height of heaven, where it blazed beautifully, illuminating the earth with its rays: it has set and left the world in gloomy darkness respecting itself; and, it is only by reflection from other satellital bodies, that we have the slightest knowledge of what it was. But perhaps in some future day, when. men are more enlightened than the present race, when science and learning have reached nearer to perfection, it will again be seen to rise in prospect; and, then, it will appear that the ancient Druidical and patriarchal religions were alike.

THE END